RESEARCH IN MENTAL ILLNESS

Research in Mental Illness

With contributions by

R S BLUGLASS · JONATHAN CHICK · JOHN CRAMMER · T J CROW
OMAR DANIELS · HUGH L FREEMAN · DOROTHY H HEARD
MALCOLM LADER · JULIAN LEFF · W A LISHMANN · ISAAC MARKS
ROBIN M MURRAY · MICHAEL PARE · DEREK RICHTER
HENRY ROLLIN · SIR MARTIN ROTH · PETER SAINSBURY
A C P SIMS · JAN STERN · J P WATSON

Edited by

DEREK RICHTER MRCP HonFRCPsych
*Formerly Director of the MRC Neuropsychiatry Unit
and Secretary-General of IBRO*

WILLIAM HEINEMANN MEDICAL BOOKS LTD

23 Bedford Square, London WC1B 3HH

First published in 1984

© Derek Richter, 1984

ISBN 0 433 27601 0

Photoset by Wilmaset, Birkenhead, Merseyside
Printed in Great Britain by
Biddles Ltd, Guildford

Contents

1	Changing Problems	1
2	Origins and Treatment of Neuroses	14
3	Psychotherapy Research	26
4	Alcohol-Related Problems	35
5	The Prevention of Suicide	48
6	Causes and Treatment of Depression	59
7	New Clinical and Laboratory Techniques	69
8	Social Influences in Schizophrenia	85
9	Causes and Treatment of Schizophrenia	97
10	Research in Child Psychiatry	107
11	Research in Mental Handicap	121
12	Mental Disorder in Old Age	135
13	Research in Forensic Psychiatry	153
14	Research in Community Care	163
	Index	173

Royalties from the sale of this book will be given in equal amounts to:

The Royal College of Psychiatrists

The Mental Health Foundation

The National Association for Mental Health (MIND)

The National Schizophrenia Fellowship

Preface

Research has played an important part in increasing our understanding of the nature and causes of mental disorders and, in so doing, it has added considerably to the available methods of treatment so that there has been a significant improvement in the outlook for the mentally ill. While this is generally appreciated in medical circles, the achievements of psychiatric research are not so widely known elsewhere, nor is it generally known that the prospects for further research leading to further advances appear to be good.

In this situation members of the Research Committee of the Royal College of Psychiatrists agreed to cooperate in the production of a small book which deals with the value of psychiatric research. The book does not attempt to be comprehensive but, in order to obtain a reasonably wide coverage of the subject, a number of leading psychiatrists were invited to contribute short accounts of investigations which have helped to extend our knowledge of various aspects of psychiatric illness. This provided a series of pictures of varying psychiatric problems and described the relevant research carried out on them. In a relatively new and developing field such as psychiatry, some variations of individual viewpoint are to be expected and it is of interest to see the diverse attitudes to some of the problems discussed in different sections of the book. However, there was general agreement on the value of the research which has been carried out hitherto and on the need for more.

Some types of modern psychiatric research are highly technical in nature, requiring an intimate knowledge, for example, of the complex mechanisms operating in the brain. Their detailed description is beyond the scope of the present book, but it could be misleading to omit them entirely and they are, therefore, described briefly in the sections in which they are relevant. But the use of technical terms has been avoided as far as possible, so that most of the book can be read without an extensive knowledge of medical science.

1
Changing Problems

Mental illness generally develops in individuals living in communities, not in isolation. This means that the changing conditions in society have an effect on the manifestation of mental illness and also on its treatment. For the majority of people in the western world, there have been significant changes in their social surroundings in recent years with a general improvement in the conditions of life. In spite of occasional recessions, hours of work have generally fallen and working people's wages have increased. No longer do we see the extremes of poverty that were common in former years. The social services have been extended and the development of radio and television networks has helped to widen horizons by bringing educational programmes and international news as well as drama and music into many homes. The general improvement in the standard of physical health is indicated by the falling infant and maternal mortality rates and the longer expectation of life. Never before have the opportunities been better for people to live full, active and rewarding lives. And yet, in spite of all the material advances that have been made, many lives are wrecked by the pain and suffering caused by mental disorders, which range from the more serious forms of illness requiring mental hospital treatment to neuroses and personality disorders that can damage personal relations and cause great unhappiness. Many people who should be enjoying life walk in misery and relationships that should be happy are spoiled.

What then can be done about this problem? The view is still widely held that mental illness is largely incurable and there is nothing that can be done about it. Is it then something that must remain with us for ever, or is it a problem that by taking suitable measures we can reasonably hope to remedy? In trying to answer this question it may be helpful to look at some of the commoner forms of mental illness, such as schizophrenia, depression, etc., and try to assess the progress that has been made hitherto through research in increasing our understanding of the nature of the condition and our ability to deal with it. We should then be in a better position to judge what hopes there may be for further progress in the future. In this connexion it is also relevant to consider the progress that has been made in diagnosing the different types of mental disorder and in providing for the management and treatment of the mentally ill, as well as for carrying out further research. But first let us consider the general state of the problem of mental illness at the present time.

The present situation

The extent of the problem of mental illness is not always appreciated by those not directly involved in the care of the mentally ill. Recent surveys in the UK have shown that one family in five is affected by mental illness of one kind or another. One man in nine and one woman in five will require psychiatric treatment at some time in their lives, and more than 30 million working days are lost through mental disorders each year. Schizophrenia alone affects about 1% of the population: this means that in every street of a hundred houses, a number equivalent on average to one whole household will develop a schizophrenic illness. A comparable number will suffer from serious depression. The total suffering caused by mental illness is disturbingly great.

In the UK some 5000 individuals kill themselves each year and it is estimated that more than 40 000 make a suicide attempt. It is now generally recognised that many suicide attempts represent a 'cry for help', or parasuicide, rather than a serious wish to die, but in either case there remains the urgent need for help. Alcoholism is a growing problem, especially in the young, and it is estimated that some 400 000 persons of both sexes in England and Wales (11 per 1000) have a serious drink problem. The trend of drug addiction appears to be upwards too. In addition, there are more than 50 000 families who have to cope with a mentally handicapped child.

The situation has changed in some respects in recent years. In the years 1949 to 1979 the population of the UK increased from 49 to more than 54 millions. A large part of this increase was in the number of those aged 65 and over, which rose from 5.2 to more than 8 millions, an increase of 56%. Associated with this change there has been a corresponding increase in those suffering from disorders of old age. The number of beds occupied by geriatric patients in mental hospitals in England and Wales now exceeds 50 000 and there are also 160 000 such beds in general hospitals and welfare homes, where it is estimated that 30% of the elderly occupants are demented or mentally confused. Statistics of this kind indicate the general extent of the problem, but a more accurate picture can be obtained if we consider in greater detail the different diagnostic categories.

Advances in diagnosis

How many people suffer from the various different kinds of mental illness? In trying to determine the incidence of specific types of mental illness in any community an important factor is the reliability of diagnosis. Diagnosis is important as an indication of the appropriate form of treatment for the patient and in allowing the psychiatrist to make a prognosis. It also allows the nurses, psychiatrists and research workers to communicate with each other and to discuss their patients' illnesses in a meaningful way.

Some diagnoses, as for example *arteriosclerotic dementia*, indicate conditions with a specific underlying pathology and point to the cause of the illness; but mental illness is recognised more often only by symptoms relating to the way in which an individual perceives, thinks, feels and behaves. The diagnosis then indicates a particular syndrome or descriptive set of symptoms by which the condition is defined. Thus, in the condition diagnosed as *anorexia nervosa*, in which the patient loses appetite and refuses to eat, a number of different physiological and psychological factors may all play a part in giving rise to the condition, and the diagnosis does not indicate a specific underlying cause. In a syndrome of this kind we can sometimes recognise subgroups in which different causal factors are of primary importance.

The various categories used in psychiatric diagnosis provide a convenient short-hand method of representing different psychiatric conditions. Since there are no hard and fast rules for the sets of symptoms defining most psychiatric diagnoses, they have varied to some extent in different countries so that in the past psychiatric diagnosis was far from reliable. In recent years the uniformity of diagnosis has been improved by the increased use of standard diagnostic manuals as a means of categorising mental disorders.[1] Standard lists and descriptions of psychiatric conditions have been included in the International Classification of Diseases (9th Revision, 1977) and the use of this standard list has greatly improved the quality of psychiatric diagnosis making it possible, for example, to determine the frequency of different psychiatric conditions in countries varying in language and in culture.[2] Thus, it is of interest to learn from research carried out under the auspices of the World Health Organization that schizophrenia is as common in Nigeria as in a suburb of London.

The descriptions of psychiatric conditions given in the

standard list of the International Classification still leave room for a good deal of individual variation in the cases included in any particular diagnostic category. For the purposes of research, where greater precision is required, it is therefore helpful to use 'operational definitions' which depend on applying a stricter set of criteria, so that the individual variation is reduced and greater uniformity is achieved.[3] The use of such operational definitions makes it easier for investigations carried out at any one research centre to be repeated elsewhere.

Another development in the classification of mental patients for research is the use of the Present State Examination (PSE). This depends on a structured interview in which an attempt is made to measure the extent of the different psychological symptoms and the general behaviour of the patient.[4] Using the PSE, it is possible to study the way in which mental illnesses vary quantitatively as well as qualitatively in different populations.

How exactly are the various forms of mental illness distributed in different sections of the community? Several investigations have shown that the incidence of schizophrenia is higher in the disorganised inner city districts than in the prosperous outer suburbs of the towns. Schizophrenia may be the diagnosis attached to as many as 60% of the inpatients in the long-stay wards of a conventional mental hospital, but it accounts for only a very small proportion (perhaps 2–3%) of patients attending psychiatric outpatient clinics. The methods used to screen different populations for mental disorders include the General Health Questionnaire, which was designed to detect symptoms of psychiatric disorder in people who go to see their general practitioner for a wide variety of other complaints.[5] By the use of such methods, information has been obtained of the frequency of the types of mental illness found in different groups in the community.

Besides the need for reliable diagnosis, the outlook for the mentally ill depends on the facilities that are available for their management and treatment, either in institutions providing nursing care or in the community.

The management of the mentally ill

In recent years there have been considerable changes in the management of the mentally ill. In 1948—over 35 years ago—the National Health Service was introduced. Britain was the first country in the world to offer free medical care to the whole population. The building up of a general health service helped to draw attention to the conditions of patients in the mental hospitals, in institutions for the mentally handicapped and in the community. There was a growing appreciation of the harmful effects of retaining patients for long periods in psychiatric institutions and the number in the mental hospitals was steadily reduced. Thus the number of patients occupying mental hospital beds in the UK fell from 143 000 in 1954 to 76 000 in 1971 and the number still continues to fall. A major factor affecting the number of patients in the mental hospitals and the conditions under which they live was the 'drug revolution' of the 1950s. The introduction of the phenothiazines and other 'antipsychotic' drugs made it possible for the behaviour of many psychotic patients to be improved sufficiently to allow them to leave hospital and live in the community. It should be clear that these patients cannot be regarded as cured: it means rather that the task of caring for them was transferred from the hospitals to the community, which must still make provision for their special needs.

Another important factor affecting the size of the mental hospital population was the development of more effective methods of treatment of manic-depressive illness. The technique of electroshock treatment (ECT) was improved, and the new tricyclic antidepressant drugs and lithium treatment were introduced. These changes enabled many former long-stay patients to leave hospital or to be admitted only for short periods. This resulted in the closure of many of the old wards for 'melancholics', which were a feature of the older mental hospitals. During the 1950s the conditions in many of the mental hospitals were considerably improved. The heavy manual work formerly given to patients was replaced by improved forms of occupational therapy and training in rehabilitation. Monetary payments were given to all patients irrespective of whether or not they worked, so that no patients were left penniless. Personal clothing of a higher standard was provided and hairdressing salons for male and female patients were introduced. For geriatric patients new methods of habit training helped to eliminate the old urine-stained floors. In some hospitals regular ward team meetings were started and the physical and mental condition of every patient was reassessed and recorded at regular intervals. Annual x-rays and TB tests were introduced both for patients and for staff. Advances of this kind were not uniformly achieved in all hospitals and in all areas and much still remains to be done, but, broadly, it can be said that the conditions of patients have generally improved and there has been a change of emphasis towards active treatment and rehabilitation, rather than just custodial care and control.

One of the effects of the Mental Health Act (1959) in the UK was to encourage the admission of patients to mental hospitals on a voluntary or 'informal' basis and by 1976 only 11.2% of patients were still admitted on compulsory orders. Most of the patients in mental hospitals now occupy unlocked wards and the general approach is much more flexible, so that inpatients can easily change to daypatients, living out of hospital and attending a Day Hospital during the day.[6] Inpatients are also encouraged to continue working in their normal employment out of hospital during the day, while still sleeping in the hospital at night. They may also go on leave to their homes.

The number of psychiatric patients living at home as daypatients or as outpatients has risen steadily. This change reflects both the advances in treatment and the greater readiness of people to receive help at an earlier stage of mental illness. While the mean length of stay in hospital has been drastically reduced, the number of admissions has increased. This is partly because of the increased willingness of people who are not so severely disturbed to accept mental hospital care. During the last twenty years the pattern of psychiatric care has changed. At one time large numbers of patients received custodial care in large institutions over long periods of time, whereas today many patients are treated for much shorter periods of perhaps only a few weeks. They may subsequently return to hospital if they relapse and, in some cases, patients return to hospital several times in what has been described as the 'revolving door' process. Admission to a mental hospital is no longer regarded as a life sentence, but rather as an opportunity for skilled reassessment and active treatment for short periods of a month or less. Those remaining permanently in hospital are mainly the older patients suffering from conditions such as dementia for which no effective treatment has, as yet, been found.

The change from custodial care to the active treatment of mental patients in mental hospitals, Day Hospitals, etc. has necessitated corresponding changes in the staffing of mental health facilities. This has been recognised in the Government publication *Better Services for the Mentally Ill*[7] in which the target set was one consultant psychiatrist for a population of 40 000 people. The optimum arrangements for the care and management of the mentally ill and for the staffing of the mental health facilities are still a matter for research.

Advances in research

In recent years there have been big advances in general medicine as, for example, in the treatment of infectious diseases, but research in mental illness has advanced a good deal less. This may be due in part to our limited understanding of the brain, which is far more complex than any other organ in the body. A more important reason for the tardiness in research in mental health is probably the fact that, for historical reasons, it has been the custom to care for the mentally ill in hospitals or asylums in outlying districts away from the medical schools, which are the main centres of medical research. Mental patients, have, therefore, not received the same attention from the medical community in general, and from research workers in particular, as those suffering from other kinds of illness.

Changing Problems

The current situation is illustrated by the small number of research workers and technical staff engaged in mental health research as compared with other branches of medicine. Although mental patients occupy some 40% of all hospital beds, it is estimated that less than 5% of medical research is devoted to research in mental health. This is again illustrated by the financial support directed from voluntary sources into medical research. A survey made by the Charities Aid Foundation in the UK has shown that only about 1% of the income raised by charities is devoted to mental health research.

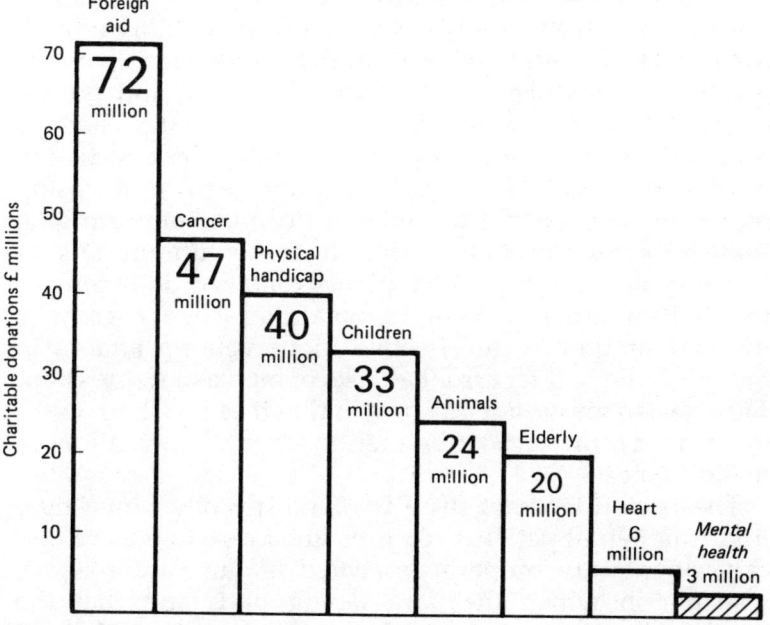

Fig. 1 Mental health: No. 1 priority.

Despite these limitations, research into the causes and treatment of mental disorders continues and some notable advances have been made in the mental hospitals equipped for such research. Patients suffering from mental disorders have also coincidentally benefited from some of the research in other fields of medicine. This applies, for example, to the use of drugs such as penicillin in the treatment of the 'toxic-infective' psychoses caused by infections. The development of the modern antipsychotic drugs started in 1952 when Delay, Deniker and Harl first used the drug chlorpromazine for the treatment of a mixed group of psychotic patients. They reported it to be better than any previously attempted drug therapy as it 'reduced both agitation and confusion'. Chlorpromazine proved to be of very great value for treating schizophrenia and now, thirty years later, it is still in use, despite the later introduction of a number of other newer related compounds. A few years later, in 1957, a notable success was achieved by the treatment of depressive illness with the drug iproniazid, which had been used for treating tuberculosis. This followed the clinical observation that tuberculous patients given this drug became cheerful and elated, and put on weight. A year later, in 1958, the tricyclic drugs, such as imipramine, were discovered to be even more effective in depression and this was an important factor in releasing many 'melancholics' from mental hospitals and bringing them back into the community. The use of lithium salts for treating manic-depressive patients followed an extensive trial in Denmark in 1954 by Schou and his colleagues, who found that they were effective in preventing attacks in patients who had recurrent attacks of mania or depression. This was an important advance in that it established one of the first prophylactic treatments for the prevention of mental illness.

The performance of drug trials or any other investigations on mental patients requires great care to ensure that the patients are properly informed of the nature of the research in which they are taking part, and that the investigations are made with their full consent. Mental health research in the UK was helped by the provision, in the mental hospitals where research is carried out, of Ethical Committees which review any research that may be planned to ensure that it is safe, scientifically sound and in the patients' best interests. Besides safeguarding the patients' interests, the Ethical Committees are also helpful in maintaining good relations with the general public by counteracting any incorrect criticisms that may be made. It has sometimes been felt mistakenly that there is a conflict between treating a patient as an individual person and making clinical observations as a basis for research hypotheses. In practice, the best of medicine combines these two factors.

Besides the advances in treatment that have been described, the increased application of the basic sciences has led to the development of valuable new biochemical, electronic, bacteriological and other techniques for the investigation of mental patients. Laboratory methods are now available for determining the blood levels of antipsychotic drugs in patients who are being treated, so that optimum levels can be maintained.

Further advances in the treatment and prevention of mental illness would appear to depend on our extending our knowledge and understanding of the working of the human brain. It was formerly believed that the transmission of impulses within the brain is exclusively an electrical phenomenon, but evidence has gradually been obtained that chemical compounds, known as neurotransmitters, are released at the nerve endings and stimulate adjacent nerve cells by acting at specific receptor sites. Chemical substances which act as transmitters in this way include acetylcholine, noradrenaline, dopamine and 5-hydroxytryptamine. There are a number of other substances located in different systems in the brain, which act as transmitters or modify transmission by influencing the receptor sites. This is now a lively field of research and its relevance to the problems of mental illness is indicated by the observation that the transmitter mechanisms are apparently the main point of action of the antipsychotic drugs. Postmortem studies by Bird and Iversen in 1977 on brain tissue from patients who had suffered from Huntington's chorea have now given direct evidence of a local defect in the transmitter mechanisms in certain regions of the brain in this condition. Furthermore, of special interest are a group of peptides which have recently been shown to act as powerful pain-killers, or which act in other ways to influence the functions of the brain. The possibility that they may be concerned in the causation of mental illness is already under investigation and the study of their mode of action poses a challenge for future research.

Mental health research encompasses a very wide field and includes the collection and interpretation of information on the effects of changes in the management and care of the mentally ill. The prognosis of mental illness is greatly affected by the social environment in which the patient lives, and the publication of the results of sociological research has helped to improve public attitudes towards mental illness so that more individuals with treatable conditions present themselves for treatment.

An example of the way in which psychiatric research has moulded both public opinion and administrative action can be seen in the studies carried out by Bowlby[8] of the effects on young children of maternal deprivation. Following the publication of the results of his investigations, more attention was given to the social structure of institutions for the care of children. There was also a change of attitude towards the taking of young children into custody, and provision was made in many hospitals for mothers to live there while their children are being treated as inpatients.

Studies of the families of mental patients have given evidence that hereditary as well as environmental factors both play a part in the causation of different kinds of mental illness. In the case of schizophrenia, for example, the risk of developing a psychosis increases with the closeness of blood relationship to a schizophrenic, and twin studies have shown a consistently higher incidence of psychosis in identical than in non-identical twins brought up in the same environment. Studies of adoptive children of schizophrenic parents have also helped to throw light on the extent to which different environmental and genetic factors operate in this condition.

The advances that have been made in the treatment of mental illness have had a significant effect on the attitude of society towards the mentally ill. It is now widely accepted that many mental and nervous disorders are treatable conditions, and with the improvement in prognosis some, at least, of the old stigma has disappeared. It may be concluded that the developments that have taken place in our general understanding of the nature of mental disorders have done much to improve the outlook for the mentally ill.

References

1. American Psychiatric Association (1981). *Diagnostic and Statistical Manual of Mental disorders*. DSM–III.
2. International Classification of Diseases (1977). *Manual of the International Statistical Classification of Diseases, Injuries and Causes of Death*. Geneva: World Health Organization.
3. Feighner J. P., Robins E., Guze S. B., Woodruff R. A., Winokur G., Munoz R. (1972). Diagnostic criteria for use in psychiatric research. *Arch. Gen. Psychiat*; **26**: 57–63.
4. Wing J. K., Cooper J. E., Sartorius N. (1974). *The Measurement and Classification of Psychiatric Symptoms*. Cambridge: Cambridge University Press.
5. Goldberg D. P. (1972). *The Detection of Psychiatric Illness by Questionnaire*. London: Oxford University Press.
6. Department of Health and Social Services (1978). *Facilities and Services of Mental Illness and Mental Handicapped Hospitals in England 1976*. London: HMSO.
7. Department of Health and Social Services (1975). *Better Services for the Mentally Ill*. London: HMSO.
8. Bowlby J. (1951). *Maternal Care and Mental Health*. Geneva: World Health Organization Monograph Series No. 2.

2

Origins and Treatment of Neuroses

Neuroses are those conditions in which the main problem is some form of anxiety or its equivalent. Worry is, of course, a perennial feature of the human condition and it can be hard to decide when to speak of normal tension and when to speak of an anxiety disorder. In general, it is customary to label problems as disorders once they start handicapping everyday activities. As an example, it is perfectly normal to have a mild fear of heights, but we speak of a phobic disorder when this is so intense that the sufferer cannot work in an office above the ground floor. Similarly, anxiety about sexual performance is natural in a first sexual experience, but if this should lead to nonconsummation of a marriage after a year, then this is a disorder warranting treatment.

Research has shown that neurotic disorders are far the commonest of all psychiatric problems in the general population, accounting for some 10 to 20% of all consultations with general practitioners. Only about one in twenty of these get referred to a psychiatrist for specialised psychiatric attention. Careful research has indicated the fallacy of the myth that neurosis is simply a product of the stress of modern living or urban civilisation. The prevalence of neurotic problems is remarkably similar in rural and in urban settings both in industrialised and in developing countries.[1]

Though the prevalence of neuroses as a whole is

similar around the world, cultural differences do produce large variations in referral patterns in different countries. There may also be variations in the prevalence of particular neurotic syndromes in different countries, e.g. conversion hysteria, in which the subject for no apparent reason suddenly loses the power of speech, hearing, sensation or movement, is commoner in less sophisticated populations. Cultural attitudes also influence whether sufferers from sexual disorders ask for help from their medical advisers.

Mental health research is now beginning to unravel certain factors which contribute to the causation of some neuroses.[2] It has been shown from research into twins and by other methods that there is a small, but tangible, genetic component to having certain excessive personality traits associated with some neuroses, e.g. timidity or meticulousness. Heredity can also predispose to the presence of phobic and obsessive-compulsive symptoms.

Another characteristic emerging from research is that people tend to develop phobias more readily to certain situations than to others, and that several of these emerge as maturational phenomena selectively at particular ages. These patterns suggest that as a species we have a built-in tendency to being frightened of natural evolutionary dangers such as heights, animals, or darkness. Similarly the phobic response to most stimuli seems to be preprogrammed. The usual reaction to most phobic situations is to have palpitations and an increase in heart rate; although phobics often *feel* faint, actual fainting is rare. In contrast, in response to the sight of blood or injury, it is more common to have a slowing of the heart rate and actual fainting.

A frequent misconception in the popular mind is that genetic or biological factors contributing to mental disorders must make them especially hard to treat. This turns out not to be the case. An important point to come out of research is the fact that despite clearcut biological contributions to the origin of certain phobias, such phobias are nevertheless eminently treatable by psychological means.

There are also environmental factors in the development of neurosis, though more research is needed before we can understand them in detail. Investigations have found an association between social isolation and neuroses like anxiety states and neurotic depression. It remains to be seen whether either comes first and to what extent they reinforce one another in a vicious circle. Having many confidants and friends seems to protect against the development of certain neuroses.

Clearcut traumas can initiate many different kinds of neuroses, just as they can many physical illnesses. This is often thought to argue for a straightforward explanation of neuroses as the products of conditioning processes, but research finds this view to be oversimplified. Only a minority of phobics give a clearcut history of traumatic conditioning. An additional small number seem to have acquired their fears, at least in part, after observing phobic relatives, so 'modelling' or 'observational learning' also has a part to play in some people. Bereavement and other losses are usually followed by normal grieving, but sometimes this is prolonged into a chronic neurotic reaction which recent workers have found can be treated successfully and also prevented.

Although understanding of the causation of neuroses is only beginning to unfold, mental health research over the last twenty years has made substantial advances which have facilitated the relief of much neurotic distress. Treatments can conveniently be divided into drugs and psychological means.

Drug treatment of neuroses

The pharmacological treatment of neuroses involves two main classes of drugs, the tranquilliser/sedatives such as diazepam (Valium) and the antidepressants such as amitriptyline (Tryptizol) and phenelzine (Nardil)[3].

Tranquillisers and sleeping tablets are the most widely used of all prescribed medicines. Tranquillisers allay anxieties, have a calming influence and reduce the unpleasant symptoms of stress responses. Sleeping tablets are similar drugs, but are given at night to help induce sleep, especially in the anxious.

The barbiturates such as butobarbitone (Soneryl) have been largely supplanted by the benzodiazepines (such as diazepam, (Valium), lorazepam (Ativan) and nitrazepam (Mogadon). This is because the benzodiazepines are generally more effective than the barbiturates (except for severe insomnia) and are much safer in overdose.

The benzodiazepines comprise about 15 drugs currently available, which can be divided into four groups depending on their actions and indications:

1. Tranquillisers with long-acting effects include diazepam, chlordiazepoxide (Librium), clorazepate (Tranxene) and medazepam (Nobrium). These drugs are long-acting and are appropriate in patients with high sustained levels of anxiety.
2. Tranquillisers with shorter durations of action, oxazepam (Serenid) and lorazepam (Ativan) are particularly useful in patients whose anxiety levels fluctuate. They can take one of these drugs when required and not experience persistent sedation.
3. Sleeping tablets with sustained actions are nitrazepam (Mogadon) and flurazepam (Dalmane). These drugs are fairly long-acting and can produce sedation the next day. They are useful in patients with sleeping problems who also need to have their anxiety allayed during the day.
4. Sleeping tablets with shorter actions are temazepam (Normison, Euhypnos) and triazolam (Halcion). They are appropriate for patients who need help to sleep, but do not want to be sedated the next day.

Many patients with anxiety attacks or bouts of insomnia recover within a few weeks whether drug treatment is given or not. It is doubtful whether tranquillisers hasten this process, although they do lessen the severity of the symptoms. However, anxiety levels become so high in some patients that they cannot cope; in such cases tranquillisers are invaluable in lessening the anxiety to manageable levels.

Both tranquillisers and sleeping tablets tend to lose their effectiveness with long-term administration. About 80% of anxious patients starting treatment on tranquillisers take them as a short course, but the other 20% are still taking them after six months. In many of these patients, the symptoms have subsided. Recent research has shown that in some long-term users a form of physical dependence may supervene. Thus, every patient whose course of tranquilliser treatment stretches out unduly should be carefully reviewed and slowly withdrawn from the drugs where appropriate.

Antidepressant drugs are commonly used in neurotic patients with depressive symptoms. Two groups of antidepressants are available, the tricyclic antidepressants (TCAs) (with 3 rings in the chemical structure) and the monoamine oxidase inhibitors (MAOIs). Some newer compounds with a variety of chemical structures, e.g. mianserin (Bolvidon, Norval) resemble the TCAs in therapeutic action, but have fewer side effects.

The TCAs are fairly effective in lessening neurotic depression, but are much more useful in patients with 'endogenous' depression. Treatment may need to be continued for some time because the drugs do not cure the illness, but suppress the symptoms. Response may be delayed and be incomplete and any associated anxiety may be even slower to resolve than the depression. TCAs have a wide range of side-effects such as dry mouth, constipation and often sedation, and are unpleasant to take.

The MAOIs are used much less frequently than the TCAs because they have more severe side-effects and are generally less effective. However, some neurotic patients such as the phobically anxious or the hypochondriacal may show a gratifying response. Patients taking these drugs must avoid cough and cold remedies and some foods such as cheese and yeast extracts. Patients who respond well to MAOIs may need to continue their medication for several months or more.

All these drug treatments for neurosis are symptomatic; i.e. they control the depressing symptoms—psychological and bodily—while other forms of therapy can be instituted and the patient's coping capabilities are mobilised.

Behavioural psychotherapy

Especially in the last decade, a major research endeavour has led to impressive advances in the treatment of neuroses by psychological means, and many sufferers can now be helped for the first time by what has come to be known as 'behavioural psychotherapy'. The behavioural revolution has led to a radical change in thinking about psychological treatment, which has led to effective new methods for helping selected problems. No longer is it necessary in every case to look back at one's childhood to get over these worries. That approach often made people feel helpless, because they could not reconstruct their life histories, and blaming parents achieves little beyond inducing burdensome guilt. Therapists used to believe in the need to uncover something in order to help. Along with this went the myth of symptom substitution, the belief that if the fear was reduced without dealing with the supposed underlying 'problem', then some other trouble would pop up in its place. Research has shown time and again that this notion is largely groundless. People who lose their phobias or rituals, far from developing fresh symptoms, usually also improve in other areas of their life as the result of being freed from the constraints formerly imposed by their fears.

Behavioural psychotherapy is an approach to modify unwanted behaviour directly by a variety of methods which share certain general principles. These include clear delineation of the treatment goals towards which the treatment is directed; cooperation of the patient towards attainment of these goals, involvement of the family where necessary, and practise by the patient of required homework assignments between sessions.

Behavioural treatments can be given to patients individually or in groups, depending on what is practicable and desirable in a given case, and they usually last from one to fifteen sessions. The treatments include (a) methods to reduce anxiety-linked behaviour such as phobias or compulsive rituals, usually by forms of exposure to the anxiety-provoking situation, (b) reduction of appetitive behaviours such as exhibitionism or obesity, by a variety of self-regulatory methods and (c) the development of new behaviour by methods such as teaching social skills to those who lack them. For example, an agoraphobic individual who fears to leave her room may be encouraged at each session to take a few more steps out each day: or a child with a phobia of birds may be taught to accept them by feeding him at first in the presence of a stuffed bird placed some distance away and later in the presence of a live bird in a cage, which is gradually brought nearer.

There is now abundant evidence that behavioural treatments work for many neuroses which were formerly untreatable. Phobic, obsessive-compulsive and sexual disorders, bed wetting, problems with social skills, stammering, morbid grief and nightmares are among those conditions which, as a result of research, have become malleable with appropriate behavioural treatment. The range of problems amenable to the behavioural approach is widening and already amounts to perhaps a quarter of all the neuroses seen in psychiatric clinics. Improvement with behavioural treatment usually continues in the years after active treatment has finished. Long-term followup has found phobics to be well up to the nine years that have so far elapsed since behavioural treatment was completed.

An important point to emerge from research is knowledge about which kinds of difficulties can be alleviated with existing methods. Not everybody can be helped. For success, the sufferer must be clear about the problem with which he wants help and must feel that he will be better off without, rather than with, the problem. He needs to be prepared to tolerate some discomfort and to cooperate actively in the treatment planned, including doing a fair amount of 'homework' on the problem. Sometimes relatives will also need to lend a hand. Obsessive-compulsive rituals can implicate the family, who then have to be enlisted as aides to the therapist, and for most sexual difficulties the partner would need to be involved in some way.

There is no mystery in the treatment principles by which phobias and rituals are reduced, although severe problems are best handled by professional therapists. It has been found that if professional aid is not available, some self-help may be possible, especially for problems which are fairly recent or mild and only need some self-management.

More and more self-help has become possible as research has worked out the principles of treatment and simplified them. This is a recurring theme in health care. Malnutrition was common in the past before doctors worked out the balanced diet we need for normal development and function. Now that nutritional principles are common knowledge, by virtue of being taught at school, covered in the media and disseminated in popular books, most people can keep themselves in a state of normal nutrition. Severe diarrhoea from whatever cause used to kill innumerable infants until it was discovered how important it is to maintain the body's fluids and salts in proper balance. Until recently, this was done by the giving of intravenous fluids, which needs medical and nursing help, but then it was found that babies with gastroenteritis can take special liquids by mouth without vomiting, thus doing away with the need to give fluids intravenously. So when there are epidemics of gastroenteritis in babies, their mothers can give them the correct fluid by mouth. The child will not vomit this, and so its stomach can absorb the liquid and its life is saved. As doctors worked out the principles of treatment and simplified the management of the problem, they could fade themselves out of the treatment and let the mothers themselves do much of the management.

A process rather like this is beginning to happen with behavioural treatment of various types of anxiety. Research in self-help is leading to the 'scientific approach to willpower' which is necessary for success. Emphasis is shifting towards patients carrying out much of their own treatment, with the therapist merely setting the course and giving a touch to the rudder at intervals. Self-help manuals are a critical aid in this process and research has culminated in such a manual becoming available for those with phobic and obsessive-compulsive difficulties.[4] Such self-help aids are one fruit of a scientific endeavour which is continuing to refine treatment methods so that they become even more effective and easy to apply in a widening range of problems.

It is worth tracing some of the effective behavioural principles which have developed as a result of research into mental health. One of the most important things to understand about anxiety is that it is perfectly normal for all of us to feel anxious from time to time. Moreover, tension can be constructive. It can spur us on to deal with the problems that are the cause of our tension. We all feel unhappy if we are stricken with serious illness, by loss of a job, by failure in important examinations, or after arguments with our wives or tiffs with our children. We may be faced with financial demands which we find hard to meet, or our car might break down on the way to an important engagement. In fact, our hardships cease only with death.

The aim is not to abolish anxiety—that can't be done. Instead people can learn to put it in perspective, to cease regarding it as an enemy and instead to recruit it as a spur to necessary action. We can learn to roll with every stress. An important aspect of stress is being able to talk about it, to ask for help when necessary from relatives or friends. Talking about our fears to someone we can trust can be valuable for some of our difficulties. This person can be a friend or a member of the caring profession. Supportive psychotherapy may be all that is needed for many people who are suffering from anxiety. In others, however, what we have now come to call 'exposure treatments' are necessary to overcome tensions which arise in repetitive situations. Exposure treatments are a form of behavioural psychotherapy.

Behavioural psychotherapy has transformed the outlook for persistent phobias and obsessive-compulsive rituals. Before then the commonest psychological approach was that derived from Freudian models of psychoanalysis and psychotherapy. These assumed that phobias and rituals usually symbolise other hidden problems which need to be discovered, and that when these were revealed through free association and worked through, the anxieties would disappear. This form of treatment is time-consuming, expensive and can go on for years. In contrast, behavioural treatments can be effective for phobias and rituals within a few days or weeks, or at most a couple of months. Behavioural treatment does not assume that phobias are symbolic transformations of hidden difficulties. It does not look for unconscious mental aberrations. Instead it regards the phobia or ritual itself as the main handicap, and tries to eliminate it directly, not by trying to uncover unconscious meanings, but by teaching the sufferer how to face those situations which trigger his discomfort, so that he can eventually come to tolerate them. A wealth of research has shown that this approach works in most cases. Even phobias which have been present for 20 years have been overcome in 3 hours of treatment, though usually 10–20 hours are necessary, spaced over sessions 1–2 hours long.

Research has found that not all behavioural methods are equally effective for the reduction of phobias and rituals. Relaxation is often called a behavioural treatment, but it does not reduce rituals or phobias. Effective behavioural treatments known under various names, have in common the principle of exposure to the situation which causes fright until the patient becomes used to it. Once we confront a fear determinedly and cease avoiding it, then it will diminish. Research has found that provided the exposure continues for long enough, anxiety eventually goes down.[5] In a lucky minority of sufferers a few minutes' exposure to the things which terrify them lead to a reduction in fears. This might be especially true for those who have not had their phobias for long and are really determined to get the better of them. More commonly, the fears start to diminish within half-an-hour after the start of exposure, even in people with very long-standing phobias and rituals. Rarely, several hours may be needed for the fear to start abating. The important point is to persevere until the anxiety starts to lessen and to be prepared to go on until it does. In general, the more rapidly the sufferer tackles his worst fears, the more quickly he recovers. The faster and longer we embrace the monster of our panic, the more rapidly it fades in our arms to become a shadow of itself; the old familiar friend of mild tension rather than the monster of terror.

Contrary to popular belief, studies have found that anxiety during exposure is not usually harmful. In the past doctors and psychologists were scared to allow patients to become very frightened because they thought serious harm would result. Now we know from research in mental health that the great majority of patients who allow themselves to experience panic eventually become unable to experience more than mild fear. If we deliberately try to panic, paradoxically the odds are that we find we cannot do so, or that we will only produce a pale reflection of the real thing. Even if severe panic does strike, it will gradually evaporate and will be less likely to return in the future. In a curious way, really effective exposure treatments for anxiety developed only once therapists learned to endure the anxiety of their patients, secure in the knowledge that it is unlikely to harm and instead can lead to their improvement.

There is the possibility that the development of this method of treatment may actually lead to prevention of the development of many fears and rituals. There may be implications for child-rearing methods which teach children not to avoid anxiety or to run away from difficult situations. There is indirect evidence that some normal childhood fears later became persistent phobias because the children did not learn the usual coping mechanisms that most parents teach naturally.

Research into neurosis has thus increased both our understanding of the origins of many types of anxiety, and also our ability to treat these effectively and allow many sufferers to help themselves. Besides behavioural psychotherapy, there are a number of other effective kinds of psychotherapeutic treatment on which research has been carried out and these are considered further in the following chapter.

References

1. Osuntokun B. O. (1983). *The seat of pleasure and pain*. World Health; **10**: 20–3.
2. McKeon J., Roa B., Mann A. (1984). Life events and personality traits in obsessive-compulsive neurosis. *Brit. J. Psychiat*; **144**: 183–9.
3. Kielholz P. (1976). Advances in the drug therapy of effective disorders. In *Advances in the Drug Therapy of Mental Illness, pp. 92–102*. Geneva: World Health Organization.
4. Marks I. M. (1980). *Living with Fear*. New York: McGraw-Hill.
5. Cohen S. D., Monteiro W., Marks I. M. (1984). Two-year follow up of agoraphobics after exposure and imipramine. *Brit. J. Psychiat*; **144**: 276–81.

3
Psychotherapy Research

Psychotherapy is a form of psychological treatment used to help a patient by inducing specific changes in his mental attitudes and beliefs. There are many different varieties of psychotherapy and the treatments that are given range widely from simple counselling and behavioural psychotherapy to the 'psychodynamic therapy' practised by psychoanalysts. Any kind of human interaction is inevitably accompanied by psychological influences and effects: this is seen for example in the placebo effects accompanying drug treatment and in the therapeutic influence of a hospital ward. Psychotherapy goes further than this and the term is generally taken to mean a course of psychological treatment arranged with definite structure, procedure and aims, which is intended to help a patient to overcome his difficulties by developing mental attitudes of a normal and healthy kind.

The structural characteristics of psychotherapy can be defined in terms of factors such as treatment length (psychotherapies may be brief or prolonged); age of patient (treatment of children, adolescents, etc.); sex (treatment of men, women, homosexual couples, etc.); and location of patients (inpatient or outpatient). Individual and group treatments differ in the number of people involved, and group treatments can be further classified in terms of the relatedness of the participants, who may be close relatives as in family therapy, or complete strangers. Much of the psychotherapy carried out at the present time requires attendance at only a small number of sessions which are completed in a relatively short period of time. Once-weekly sessions are the average arrangement for psychotherapy in the National Health Service in the UK, but psychotherapy of the psychoanalytical type developed by Siegmund Freud requires five 50-minute sessions a week for a period that may last for several years.

For the purposes of research, the nature of any psychological treatment under investigation must be clearly defined and the procedure used by the therapist must, therefore, be specified. The interaction between therapist and patient may be regarded as having two main components, which can be called 'human' and 'professional'. The human component depends, in part, on the ability of therapist and patient to communicate meaningfully with each other and to understand each other on the basis of categories derived from ordinary life and applied habitually to other human beings. Important also is the psychotherapist's ideology, which determines the attitudes, values, expectations and intentions which he has about his work. Therapist and patient may both experience feelings of warmth, anxiety and concern about the patient's problems, but the 'professional' component exercised by the therapist modifies the normal human interaction and introduces a relationship of a one-sided kind. As the self-disclosure by the patient focusses attention on the patient's special problems, the therapist tries to understand their nature and then exercises professional skill in choosing from the wide range of conceptual systems applicable to behaviour those that make personal sense to him and which he can, therefore, advance with confidence as likely to help the patient and provide for the patient's special needs. Psychotherapy is not simply something 'done to' a patient, but an activity in which help-giver and help-seeker engage in a mutual interchange focussing on the patient's difficulties. In treatments of psychoanalytical type, the patient generally lies on a couch and 'free associates', or says what is going on in his mind, while the analyst seeks to understand the state of organisation of the patient's mental processes and then helps him to develop new ways of thinking which will enable him to overcome his difficulties. In view of the complexity of the therapist-patient interaction and the uniqueness of every individual case, it is evident that psychotherapeutic treatments cannot be defined as specifically as, for example, in drug trials, where every patient receives the identical drug in a precisely measurable dose.

In planning research to determine the most effective forms of treatment for dealing with different types of mental problems, it is also necessary to define the way in which the outcome of the treatment is to be assessed, and this raises further problems of a special kind. How, for example, should we assess the value of the treatment in the case of a man initially presenting with impotence, who attends for treatment with his wife from whom he separates as treatment ends, leaving him well pleased to have regained his potency, but her displeased at having lost her husband? Difficult cases of this kind, which are not so infrequent, emphasise the need for the desired effects of the treatment to be clearly defined. The criteria commonly used to determine outcome include (a) the clinical evaluation of symptom intensities, (b) social measures of occupational or domestic adjustment, (c) administrative data on length of stay in hospital or readmission and (d) how the recipient himself judges his treatment. It is also necessary to state the timing of the changes resulting from treatment, since the short-term changes observed during the individual therapeutic sessions or immediately post-treatment may differ from the long-term outcome recorded on follow up at a later date.

Marital problems are a common cause of mental distress. In a study of the patients referred by their GPs to a psychiatric outpatient clinic Swan and Wilson[1] found that of 69 married patients of 16 to 65 years of age who were living with their spouses and who had no previous history of psychiatric treatment, no less than 17 admitted that they were having marital or sexual difficulties for which they wished to have help. A number of investigations of marital problems have shown a strong association between marital disharmony and neurotic depression. In some cases the marital disharmony may be a consequence of the husband or wife suffering from depression, but the work of Brown et al.[2] in London strongly suggests that the depression is generally the result of an unsatisfactory marital relationship. They found that 38% of women without a close, intimate relationship with a husband or boy-friend developed psychiatric symptoms of predominantly depressive type when exposed to a severely stressful life event or a major difficulty. In cases presenting with depressive symptoms of this kind, antidepressant drug treatment is often given by the GPs, but several investigations have shown that for depressive disorders in general, a combination of drug treatment and psychotherapy is usually more effective than either form of treatment alone. The value of group therapy for patients attending a psychiatric outpatient clinic was examined by Bloch and Reibstein[3] who found in a study of 33 patients aged 20 to 39 attending weekly for group therapy sessions of 90 minutes that the most important therapeutic factor in their treatment was the gain in self-understanding, which they obtained through confrontation, feedback or interpretation by the group (including the therapist). Important also were their learning from personal interactions and the act of self-disclosure in revealing personal information to the group.

It is well known that certain drug treatments sometimes produce undesirable side-effects. Transitory negative changes are also observed from time to time during psychotherapy. Generally such negative changes have disappeared by the time the treatment is brought to an end, but an investigation by Hadley and Strupp[4] of the results of psychotherapy showed that that is not always the case. The replies they obtained from a group of 70 psychotherapists, who were using a variety of different behavioural, psychodynamic and other types of treatment, gave evidence that as many as 3 to 6% of the patients they had treated had suffered a deterioration attributable to the therapy given. Thus the therapy given to a patient with a personality disorder, for example, could result in a state of anxiety and depression, so that the patient became worse, and not better, as a result of the treatment given. A different approach to the problem of negative effects resulting from psychotherapy was recently made by Buckley et al.[5] who investigated a group of 97 psychotherapists preselected as having themselves received a course of personal psychotherapy or psychoanalysis. While the results of treatment reported by this group were positive in general, with changes involving factors such as improved interpersonal relations and enhancement of self-esteem, 21% reported that their treatment had resulted also in harmful effects, such as withdrawal from the outside world, impulsive overactivity or marital disharmony. Further research summarised by Crown[6] has led to the same conclusion, that a small proportion of the patients receiving psychotherapy are, in fact, made worse by the treatment they receive. Recent studies of the causes of the negative effects of psychotherapy have led to the conclusion that the most important source of negative effects lies in the patient, who may lack the necessary motivation or desire to change. Negative effects attributable to other factors such as lack of judgment on the part of the psychotherapist, the use of inappropriate techniques or unsatisfactory therapist-patient interaction are rare. The general conclusion, based on a considerable body of research, is that the great majority of patients receiving psychotherapy are significantly helped by the treatment they receive, and many patients are enabled thereby to live fuller and happier lives.

Despite the difficulties presented by research in this field, there have been a number of investigations aimed at studying the relative merits of different psychotherapeutic procedures in treating patients of different types. A recurrent theme is the effect on treatment and on outcome of influences such as the personal qualities of the therapist and the motivational characteristics of the patient, which are described in detail by Garfield and Bergin.[7] The aim is to clarify which kinds of treatment help which sorts of patients in which ways and in which circumstances. This has led to the identification of long lists of factors which may influence the psychotherapeutic processes and their outcomes.

A relatively common cause of mental distress is compulsive behaviour such as is seen, for example, in the compulsive gambler, and this condition has often been treated by aversive therapy, in which thoughts of gambling are associated with an unpleasant stimulus such as an electric shock. There is evidence that compulsive behaviour is attributable to a state of arousal evoked by excitatory stimuli operating in certain situations, and McConaghy and his colleagues have recently investigated the treatment of compulsive gamblers by an 'imaginal desensitisation' procedure in which the level of arousal is reduced by getting the patient to visualise the arousal situation repeatedly when in a state of complete mental and physical relaxation.[8] In a controlled study of 20 compulsive gamblers who had asked for treatment to reduce their urge to gamble, one half received this type of imaginal desensitisation treatment, while the other half agreed to be treated by aversive therapy. It was found that those treated by the imaginal desensitisation procedure showed a significantly greater reduction of the gambling urge and of gambling behaviour than was achieved in those treated by aversive therapy, and the change in behaviour persisted for a year or more after treatment. The investigators suggest that imaginal desensitisation should be tried as a method of treatment for compulsive homosexual behaviour and other forms of compulsive behaviour for which aversive therapy is generally used, as it might prove to be a more effective form of treatment for these conditions. It would appear that this is a field in which further research could be rewarding.

It is now widely accepted that a considerable proportion of the patients who visit their GPs, including many who present with physical symptoms are, in fact, suffering from psychological problems, and a number of epidemiological studies have provided convincing evidence of this. For the practising physician the first step towards treatment is diagnosis, and in different patients he may recognise a variety of emotional problems associated with anxiety, depression, social difficulties and stress-related conditions of different kinds. Where there is evidence of serious psychiatric illness, the natural course is to get the help and advice of specialists in the psychiatric services, but referral to the hospital setting can have several disadvantages. These may include delay before the patient is seen and dealt with, poor communication between the clinicians concerned, the number of different personnel who may become involved in the patient's care and the stigma of psychiatric labelling which may be associated with the referral. Clearly, there are many cases in which for reasons of this kind referral to the usual psychiatric services is inappropriate and if possible it is better that the patient should remain in the practitioner's care. The physician may be able to help by giving some reassurance, but he may have neither the time nor the experience to attempt to practise psychotherapy to any great extent. In these circumstances the pressure to prescribe a tranquilliser or an antidepressant drug is very great, and so the patient is likely to receive drug medication which may continue for a considerable time, with the associated disadvantages of the risk of overdosage and undesirable side-effects including dependence.

There have now been several investigations of experimental attempts to extend the use of psychotherapy in general practice by introducing clinical psychologists and counsellors into the primary health care teams.[9] The general idea is that they should work closely together with the practitioner in caring for his patients by discussing their problems with them and using whatever forms of psychotherapy may be required. While there is opposition in some quarters to the attachment of psychologists and counsellors to health care teams, Marie Johnstone, of the Royal Free Hospital, has shown in a study of the effects of doing so that the advantages of such an attachment include making psychological help available for many patients who cannot attend the central clinic owing to difficulties relating to travel, work, physical disability or even a presenting problem such as 'agoraphobia', or fear of venturing out. Other advantages are that the psychologist may be able to see the patient earlier, before the problems become too entrenched, and by seeing the patients in their home setting, the psychotherapy given can be made more relevant to the patients' immediate problems. The stigma for the patient is also reduced.

In a study undertaken by Zander a group of patients seen in general practice and presenting with insomnia were treated by being given a course of relaxation instruction. It was found that nearly all the patients showed a marked improvement in their sleeping habits, and most of them were delighted not to have been prescribed hypnotics (although that is what many of them had requested) when they were told that there was an alternative treatment available for them. A more extensive project undertaken by Dr Pamela Ashurst was designed to offer counselling on a random basis to a proportion of patients who had consulted their GPs for a neurotic disorder and had been prescribed psychotropic drugs, or for whom drugs had been considered, or thought to be unnecessary. The random allocation of patients to the counselled group thus made counselling help available to a group of patients for whom the GPs might not otherwise have considered it on clinical grounds. The doctors who participated in the study differed widely in their attitudes to minor neurotic disorders, so that the frequency with which psychotropic drugs were prescribed and the quantities prescribed varied considerably from one doctor to another. An independent assessment of the value of the counselling by non-medical counsellors made after one year concluded that doctors and patients both found it to be helpful, and the proportion of patients in the counselled group still receiving tranquillisers and antidepressants was about half that in the non-counselled control group. The counselling help made a dramatic difference to the lives of some patients, and a marginal difference to others. Although counselling is not the answer to all problems or applicable to all patients, it offers benefits to selected patients which make it a valuable addition to the treatment available in general practice. The further elucidation of the optimum kind of counselling intervention for which types of patients and for which problems poses an important task for further research.

References

1. Swan M., Wilson L. J. (1979). Sexual and marital problems in a psychiatric out-patient population. *Brit. J. Psychiat*; **135**: 310–4.
2. Brown G. W., Bhrolchain M. N., Harris T. (1975). Social class and psychiatric disturbance among women in an urban population. *Sociology*; **9**: 225–54.
3. Bloch S., Reibstein J. (1980). Perceptions by patients and therapists of therapeutic factors in group psychotherapy. *Brit. J. Psychiat*; **137**: 274–8.
4. Hadley S. W., Strupp H. H. (1976). Contemporary views of negative effects in psychotherapy. *Arch. Gen. Psychiat*; **33**: 1291–302.
5. Buckley P., Karasu T. B., Charles E. (1981). Psychotherapists view their personal therapy. *Psychotherapy: Theory, Research and Practice*; **18**: 299–305.
6. Crown S. (1983). Contradictions and dangers of psychotherapy. *Brit. J. Psychiat*; **143**: 436–41.
7. Garfield S. L., Bergin A. E. (1978). *Handbook of Psychiatry and Behaviour Change: An Empirical Analysis*. 2nd edn. New York: Wiley.
8. McConaghy N., Armstrong M. S., Blaszczynski A., Allcock C. (1983). Controlled comparison of aversive therapy and imaginal desensitization in compulsive gambling. *Brit. J. Psychiat*; **142**: 366–72.
9. Clare A. W., Lader M. (1982). *Psychiatry and General Practice*. London: Academic Press.

4
Alcohol-Related Problems

Research has made far reaching contributions to this important area of public health concern. Indeed, both our current ways of conceiving of alcoholism and our methods of treatment have been directly derived from new information provided by research.[1-7] Twenty years ago many doctors regarded alcoholism as a distinct disease entity which affected only a relatively small number of individuals in our society. Furthermore, they believed that the frequency of alcoholism had little to do with the way in which the remainder of the population drank. But those views can no longer be held today. Firstly, the idea that alcoholism is a disease has been widely challenged. Prolonged alcohol abuse can undoubtedly cause physical disease, but so too can overeating or bad driving, which are not diseases themselves, but are generally regarded as bad habits. In fact, it has become increasingly evident that what was formerly regarded as one disease really consists of three related components. These are (a) the adverse consequences of drinking, (b) dependence on alcohol (or alcohol addiction), neither of which can develop without (c) excessive drinking.

Thinking in this way has enabled psychiatrists to be much more specific about their patients' problems. For instance, instead of using the ill-defined and unpleasantly stigmatising term 'alcoholic', we can now talk more specifically about what alcohol-related damage one of our patients has incurred, and whether he is dependent on alcohol or not. Furthermore, this manner of thinking forced clinicians to consider what levels of drinking are dangerous, and what the relationship is between the amount the average person drinks in any country and the number of his fellow citizens who develop drinking problems.

The political implications of research

Research into these questions was pioneered by the Canadians Schmidt and de Lindt, whose work was most revealing. They found that in every society where the data were available there was a direct relationship between the annual per capita consumption (i.e. what the average citizen drinks) and the death rate from cirrhosis of the liver (a good index of the prevalence of alcohol-induced physical damage). Thus, in countries such as France and West Germany where the per capita consumption is high, then so is the death rate from cirrhosis. Furthermore, during prohibition in the USA and during both world wars in France, both overall consumption and deaths from cirrhosis declined.

The opposite has happened in postwar Britain. As can be seen in Table 1, between 1951 and 1976 the per capita alcohol consumption in England and Wales increased by 83% from 5·3 to 9·7 litres of absolute alcohol per year. As a direct consequence, there was a dramatic rise in deaths from cirrhosis, in arrests for drunkenness, and in hospital admissions for alcoholism.

Thus, the overall consumption levels in any society determine the number of casualties. The next question is what determines the overall levels of consumption, and here too research has helped to provide the answer. Research by the World Health Organization has shown that the major determinants of per capita consumption appear to be the price and availability of alcohol. Wherever alcohol is cheap and widely available, as in many Mediterranean countries, then per capita consumption and problem drinking are high. The inverse relationship of consumption

Table 1

THE INCREASE IN ALCOHOL-RELATED PROBLEMS

	1951	1976
Admissions to psychiatric hospitals with alcoholism	512	13,722
Deaths from cirrhosis	1,117	1,887
Proven drunkenness offences	53,676	108,698
Per capital annual consumption of absolute alcohol (litres)	5·3	9·7

with price can be seen by examining recent British experience. Since the immediate postwar period the relative price of alcohol (i.e. as a proportion of average wages) has steadily declined. A bottle of whisky may not seem cheap, but if it had increased at the same rate as bread, then it would now cost three times more than it actually does. This relative cheapness means, of course, that the average man (or woman) can now afford to drink much more alcohol than he or she could in the 1940s.

But, in addition, the alcohol is much easier to obtain in Britain today. The development of off-licence and supermarket outlets has resulted in much increased availability of alcohol. Wherever this has happened (most spectacularly in Finland) it has been accompanied by an increase in alcohol consumption and in the rate of problems as indicated by deaths from cirrhosis, admissions to hospital with alcoholism, and drunkenness arrests.

Thus, epidemiological research has demonstrated that the rates of alcohol dependence and alcohol-induced problems in any society can be influenced by government policies. This is, of course, quite different from the situation in regard to other psychiatric disorders. Governments cannot, for example, knowingly manipulate the rates of schizophrenia or depression. But there can no longer be any doubt that government policies on licensing and taxing alcohol have a major influence on the prevalence of alcohol-related problems. It can, therefore, be seen that alcoholism is not simply a medical problem; it is also a social and political one. Society and its agent, the government, has the power to balance the level of enjoyment the majority of its citizens get from alcohol against the number of casualties. This level can be set low, as in Saudia Arabia where there is little alcohol-induced pleasure and there are few casualties, or high as in France where the reverse is true. But these are issues for society as a whole to decide, not simply for doctors.

Problems associated with excessive drinking

Having shown that there is a relationship between average consumption levels of alcohol and the prevalence of alcohol-induced problems, researchers then looked at the question of what is a safe level of drinking. This cut-off point for safety is rather difficult to determine, but recent research has suggested that the upper limit of safe drinking for men is about 80 g of alcohol daily. This is the equivalent of about 4 pints of beer, 4 doubles of Scotch, one bottle of wine or two-thirds of a bottle of sherry. Below this level of drinking problems are unlikely, but some people are more susceptible than others and the more an individual strays above it, the more likely he is to develop problems. The safe level for women may be rather lower than for men.

What exactly are the problems that he (or she) may develop? Firstly there is alcohol dependence. Whereas the ordinary drinker varies his consumption from day to day, research has shown that the dependent individual drinks to relieve or avoid withdrawal symptoms; thus, the more dependent he is, the more alike each day's drinking becomes, and the more drinking takes precedence over other activities. His increasing tolerance enables him to sustain an alcohol intake which would incapacitate the average man, but he becomes liable to withdrawal symptoms after 8–12 hours abstinence. Consequently, each morning he may experience shaking of the hands, nausea often leading to retching, intense sweating and some anxiety and agitation. These symptoms are all rapidly, though temporarily, 'cured' by further alcohol, so consequently he finds himself unable to stop drinking. This total picture has come to be known in the past decade as the 'alcohol dependence syndrome'.

Nearly all alcohol dependent individuals also suffer from other alcohol-related disabilities, but many others have disabilities caused by alcohol even though they are not dependent on it. The disabilities can be divided into three broad groups, as shown in Table 2, physical, psychological and social. The social and psychological disabilities have been known for a long time and here the major advance in our understanding has been the realisation of just how frequent they are, and how they often precede the physical

Table 2

ALCOHOL-RELATED PROBLEMS

Social:
　Family disruption
　Employment problems
　Accidents
　Crime
　Vagrancy

Psychological:
　Mood disturbance
　Personality and intellectual deterioration
　Sexual dysfunction
　Delirium tremens
　Hallucinations
　Black-outs
　Suicide

Physical:
　Cirrhosis
　Gastritis and ulcers
　Pancreatitis
　Anaemia
　Neuropathy
　Infections
　Fetal Alcohol Syndrome

disabilities by many years. Doctors have realised that no great kudos is attached to diagnosing as a problem drinker the pot-bellied and jaundiced patient who visibly shakes as he breathes stale beer across their surgery desk. But it takes great skill to spot the alcohol abuser a decade earlier, and here these social and psychological disabilities are of great help.

The most thorough investigation into detecting alcohol abusers was carried out by a Manchester GP, Rodney Wilkins, who interviewed all individuals in his practice who he considered 'at risk' by virtue of factors associated with alcoholism. This study shows how quite simple and inexpensive research may be of great practical value. From a practice of 12 000 Wilkins identified 155 problem drinkers. His 'at risk' factors were the following:

1 *Marital difficulties*, which are all too often a consequence of heavy drinking. A wife may complain merely of her husband's boastfulness, pseudosexuality and unreality, or more seriously of violence towards herself or the children.
2 *Problems at work*. Alcohol abusers lose at least two and a half times as many days off work as their more sober workmates.
3 *Accidents*. Problem drinkers are much more liable to accidents at home, at work and on the roads. One in three drivers killed in road traffic accidents in the UK has a blood alcohol level above the legal limit.
4 *An affected relative*. Problem drinking is above all else a family condition. In the male relatives of alcohol abusers 25% have a similar problem.
5 *Certain occupations* which appear to predispose to heavy drinking (*see below* and Table 3).
6 *Mental and physical disorders* known to be associated with alcoholism.

Medical research has greatly advanced our knowledge of the physical consequences of excessive drinking. The most wellknown complication is, of course, cirrhosis of the liver. Indeed, Jellineck, the father of scientific research into

Table 3

LIVER CIRRHOSIS MORTALITY IN ENGLAND AND WALES

	Standard mortality ratio
Average occupation	100
Publicans, innkeepers	1576*
Ships officers	781
Barmen & barmaids	633
Fishermen	595
Hotelliers	506
Finance agents	392
Restauranteurs	385
Cooks	354
Authors and journalists	314
Medical practitioners	311

*A Standard Mortality Ratio of 1576 means that individuals in this occupation are more than 15 times as likely to die of cirrhosis than the average man.

alcoholism, used the death rate from cirrhosis as a measure of the prevalence of alcoholism in any community. Several studies have recently shown that, while in the 1940s only about 10% of cirrhosis in Britain was due to excessive drinking, by the 1970s the figure was over 70%. This rise is attributable to the marked increase in alcohol consumption over this period.

One popular misconception which has been disproved recently is the idea that a good diet protects against liver injury. This notion was largely derived from studies of malnourished 'Skid Row' alcoholics in the USA, whose condition improved after admission to hospital with reinstitution of a nutritious diet. While malnutrition may contribute to liver damage, many patients with severe liver disease have a more than adequate dietary intake. It is now clear that it is the alcohol intake itself which causes the liver damage.

Another recent line of enquiry has been the effect of

alcohol abuse on the brain. It has, of course, been known for many years that a small minority of chronically dependent drinkers develop a severe dementia known as Korsakoff's Syndrome, in which they are unable to remember any new information; but it used to be thought that most people diagnosed as alcoholics had intact brains. Recent research in Britain and elsewhere suggests that this may not be true. This work has made use of the new technique of computerised axial tomography (CAT scan) developed by EMI, which produces a three dimensional picture of a patient's brain. This has shown that many of those alcohol dependent individuals who psychiatrists pass as normal on their ordinary clinical testing show evidence of some brain shrinkage on the CAT scan. Furthermore, the development of more sensitive ways of testing intellectual capacities has demonstrated that many of the same individuals show minor deficits which may impair their judgement. This work has important implications. If alcohol abusers with intact brains are unable to stop drinking, it is asking a great deal to expect those whose judgement is impaired by brain damage to do so.

The other area of physical damage which has attracted recent attention concerns possible damage to the fetus. As early as 1834 a House of Commons Committee had commented that infants born to mothers who drank very heavily had 'a starved, shrivelled and imperfect look'. However, apart from a few sporadic reports, everyone appeared to forget about the possibility of alcohol damaging the fetus. However in 1972 Jones and his colleagues in Seattle began to report abnormalities in the babies of mothers who were heavily dependent on alcohol. There can now be no doubt that the 'Fetal Alcohol Syndrome' exists and is characterised by head and face deformities, stunting of growth and a risk of mental retardation and other congenital abnormalities.

The fullblown Fetal Alcohol Syndrome is quite rare and occurs only in the offspring of very heavy drinkers. Current controversy centres on whether it is merely the tip of an iceberg. Is it the extreme end of a whole range of less obvious abnormality among the children of mothers who drank, but not heavily enough to produce the fullblown syndrome? This question has not been satisfactorily answered yet, so it is difficult to advise pregnant women about what the risks are. The National Institute of Alcoholism and Alcohol Abuse in the USA states that more than two drinks a day throughout pregnancy is dangerous. But, on the other hand, the Royal College of Psychiatrists recently claimed 'a couple of bottles of wine taken each day is getting into the danger area'. Clearly this is an area in which ongoing research has yet to come up with a definitive answer.

The causes of alcoholism

We have already pointed out that non-specific factors such as the price and availability of alcohol help to set the overall prevalence of alcoholism in any society. National culture is, of course, also important. Wherever rates of alcoholism have been analysed by ethnic groups, the rates for those of Irish origin have been found to be high and those of Jews to be low. Why this should be has attracted a great deal of attention. Perhaps the most plausible theory is that which attributes the high Irish rates to the ambivalence shown to alcohol in Irish society—heavy drinking is condemned as immoral by one major section and lauded by the remainder. In contrast, surveys have shown that Jews are introduced early to alcohol and taught to drink in moderation, but subject to a strict taboo against drunkenness. Thus Jewish society avoids establishing attitudes — common elsewhere—equating the ability to drink heavily with the achievement of manhood.

Data collected by the Office of Population Censuses and Surveys has shown that certain occupations have more than their fair share of alcoholics (Table 3). At particular risk are those concerned in the manufacture, distribution and sale of alcohol, seamen, journalists, business executives and commercial travellers, those in the armed forces, and doctors. A recent study by Martin Plant and his colleagues illustrated some of the factors involved. They studied a series of new recruits to the brewing industry in Edinburgh and compared their drinking habits with those of men starting work in other industries. The former were much heavier drinkers, suggesting that individuals on their way to developing a drinking problem are selectively attracted to the drink industry. Plant and his colleagues then followed up both sets of men for two years, and reported that the consumption levels of the first group continued to increase as long as they stayed in the drink industry. This demonstrates that one of the predisposing occupational factors is the ready availability of cheap or free alcohol. Other factors may include the absence of supervision at work, and mobility with consequent estrangement from the stabilising influences of home life.

But none of the above factors explain exactly why only certain individuals develop drinking problems. Why, for instance, are only some Irish barmen alcohol abusers, while others subject to the same cultural and occupational influences continue to drink in a normal fashion? Family background is perhaps the strongest predisposing factor, and for many years it was thought that this was due to imitation rather than inheritance with abnormal attitudes being passed on through the family culture. However, recent studies have suggested that there may also be a genetic factor. Donald Goodwin and his colleagues studied the sons of alcoholics who had been adopted soon after birth and raised by normal families, and showed that they had a much higher risk of alcoholism in later life than a control group of adoptees with no biological history of alcoholism. This study is a very good example of a research project challenging widely held beliefs, and although its conclusions are not yet absolutely confirmed, it has reopened a whole area of investigation which others had regarded as irrelevant.

In contrast, systematic enquiry has helped to bury the notion that there is a 'universal alcoholic personality'. Many lay people and not a few professionals have the idea that all those with drinking problems have basically inadequate or psychopathic personalities. The trouble is that by the time such an individual comes for treatment it is difficult to distinguish personality features consequent on excessive drinking from those which were previously present. However, one recent American study compared personality profiles of individuals coming to an alcohol treatment clinic with their previous scores at college more than a decade previously. The early scores were not deviant; the later ones indicated excessive dependency. Thus, as the severity and chronicity of a drinking problem advances, the personality may coarsen and the drinker may be falsely labelled as suffering from psychopathy.

Efficacy of treatment

Approaches to treatment have benefited from research in two main ways. Firstly, pharmacological advances have resulted in more effective management of the withdrawal syndrome which dependent individuals experience when they stop drinking. This syndrome used to be a considerable hazard and before the last war some centres reported that over 5% of their severe cases died. This is no longer a problem, partly because drugs like Heminevrin and Valium given prophylactically can generally prevent the really severe symptoms such as hallucinations and convulsions developing.

The other area of benefit concerns the evaluation of different treatment approaches. 'Treatment' has always been notoriously difficult, and the management of dependence has not kept pace with advances in the treatment of its medical complications. Indeed, recent research has begun to question the value of many of the components of traditional treatment regimes. Much of this work has been carried out by Professor Griffith Edwards and his team at the Maudsley Hospital in London. Initially, these workers randomly allocated half the patients who came to their clinic to inpatient treatment and half to (the less expensive) outpatient care. When they followed up the two groups they found no difference in outcome. Subsequently, Edwards and his colleagues compared the relative merits of a single counselling session with the standard treatment offered to married men who presented to their clinic. A year later those who had had the single counselling session were doing as well as those who had had the more intensive programme of treatment.

Research like this has had considerable effect on national health service policies. Since intensive inpatient treatment appears to be less cost-effective than more simple methods, less emphasis is now being given to building more specialist inpatient units. Instead, the emphasis is on training those professionals (e.g. general practitioners and social workers) involved at the primary care level in order that they may give more simple and inexpensive help at an earlier stage in the drinker's life. This shifting of emphasis should leave the specialist inpatient units able to treat more patients, but for briefer periods, e.g. a two week admission for 'drying out' rather than a three month admission for group psychotherapy.

A number of time honoured myths have tended to impede progress towards developing effective therapies for alcohol abusers. One of these was the notion that 'once an alcoholic, always an alcoholic', which implied that life-long abstinence was the only option. This is, of course, the view of Alcoholics Anonymous and until recently was the basis of all treatment offered in the National Health Service. The first serious challenge to this 'abstinence concept' came in 1962 when Dr David Davies reported that 7 out of 93 appropriately treated alcoholic patients had returned to social drinking after a short period of abstinence in hospital. This report initially created a furore, but has since been confirmed many times by other investigations such as that by the Rand Corporation in the USA.

Thus, this line of research has revolutionised thinking about treatment options, and now several centres have research programmes in which alcohol abusers are taught how to modify the amount and rate at which they drink. It would be a foolhardy psychiatrist who would advise all his patients that they attempt to return to social drinking. Nevertheless, the possibility of teaching controlled drinking can no longer be ignored. It may be that in the future different types of alcohol abusers will be offered different treatment programmes ranging from total abstinence to social drinking.

References

1. Armor D. J., Polich J. M., Stambul H. B. (1976). *Alcoholism and Treatment*. Santa Monica, California: Rand Corporation.
2. Hore B. (1976). *Alcohol Dependence*. London: Butterworths.
3. Plant M. A. (1979). *Drinking Careers*. London: Tavistock.
4. Robinson D. (1976). *From Drinking to Alcoholism: A Sociological Commentary*. London: Wiley.
5. Royal College of Psychiatrists. (1979). *Alcohol and Alcoholism*. London: Tavistock.
6. Wilkins R. H. (1974). *The Hidden Alcoholic in General Practice*. London: Elck Sciences.
7. World Health Organization. (1977). *Alcohol-Related Disabilities*. Geneva: WHO (Offset Publication No. 32).

5
The Prevention of Suicide

Why do so many people commit suicide? Suicide raises questions to which psychiatrists, social scientists, philosophers and theologians have all proposed a variety of answers and much of the older literature on suicide deals with their different views. Research on suicide and attempted suicide, particularly in the last ten to twenty years, has now begun to ascertain the facts and provide answers based on carefully collected evidence. Clearly any causal theory of suicide must take account of the social findings and the evidence that social stresses that afflict the individual, such as bereavements or separations, can predispose to suicide; but the psychiatric findings also indicate that with few exceptions people who commit suicide have a recognisable mental disorder, and this is generally a depressive illness.[1] This conclusion is supported by clinical and epidemiological investigations along three different lines.

The first of these is based on a variation of the conventional diagnostic psychiatric interview, in which relatives and friends of suicides are interrogated soon after the act—a procedure closely akin to that followed in outpatients when the patient is too disturbed to answer questions. This technique was first used by Eli Robins in St Louis. He concluded from the psychiatric histories he obtained that 94% of 134 suicides he investigated were mentally ill and that 45% suffered from a manic-depressive disorder. A similar 'clinical postmortem' of suicides undertaken in Seattle indicated much the same incidence. In England, Barraclough recorded standardised social as well as clinical information on 100 consecutive suicides, also obtained by visiting their relatives; but in addition he interviewed a sample of 150 people of the same age and sex from the general population with whom he compared them. Further, their general practitioners also described the medical care they had given the suicides and their living controls in the previous year.

The clinical and other information was then passed to a panel of three psychiatrists who were asked to decide whether the cases had a mental illness, and if so what their diagnoses were. The panel agreed that 93% had a definite mental disorder and that in 64% this was a straightforward primary depressive illness. This figure increased to 77% if they included those suicides whose principal diagnosis was alcoholism, but who also had a manifest depressive illness as well. Most of the 64% of depressions were of the *endogenous* type, which means the kind of depression in which constitutional factors are specially important and play a large part. In order to find out whether depressives who commit suicide differ from living ones, they were compared with 128 endogenous depressives drawn at random from the same population as the suicides. The severity of the 15 depressive symptoms was the same for both; they differed from one another in only three respects: persistent insomnia, self neglect, and impaired memory, which were more evident among the suicides. The severe sleeplessness is important, because it was found that on this account many of the suicides had been prescribed the potentially lethal barbiturate hypnotics, and had then used these tablets to end their lives.

Other investigators have also compared depressives who died by suicide with depressives admitted to hospital (a more selected group) and reported the suicide cases to be more severely depressed. But the main feature which distinguished the suicides in each study is that they had made many more previous attempts at suicide—41% as compared with 4% in Barraclough's investigation. Other clinical observations which distinguish the depressive who commits suicide and which are, therefore, indicators of their being at greater risk for this act, are that they are more likely to kill themselves in the months immediately following their discharge from hospital; that they have been ill longer; and that they are more frequently male, older and separated from wife or husband. Their social circumstances differed too in that the suicides were more often socially alienated and living alone than the living depressives, and they had also suffered more recent adversities, notably bereavements.

The two groups did not differ in the number of previous episodes of depression nor in their family history of mental illness, but their similarity in these respects increased the likelihood that the retrospectively made diagnoses of depression in the suicides were valid. In both groups the figures were similar to those obtained in surveys and genetic studies of patients with endogenous depression; for example 20% of the first degree relatives had had an affective (emotional state) disorder and 6% had also died by suicide. The most pertinent findings, however, are that more than half the suicides have been shown to have an easily recognisable and treatable depressive illness, and that their depression has some distinctive clinical and social characteristics that help to identify them as being at risk for suicide. Since depression is a treatable condition, the corollary of these observations is that there is considerable scope for preventive action.

The second line of research which supports the contention that most suicides occur in the course of a depressive illness, which can be readily diagnosed and treated, are studies in which a 'cohort' of patients with carefully diagnosed depressions are followed up for a number of years and the causes of any deaths among them are established. A consistent finding is that about 1 in 6 will die by suicide. Thus in a recent review of 30 follow-up studies, which incidentally included 7 cohorts of 'neurotic depressives' as well as cohorts of primary depressives in whom the predisposition to swings of mood is to a greater extent 'built-in', the author concluded that some 15% of depressives will ultimately die by suicide.

Another kind of epidemiological research of particular value are surveys in which the mortality of a whole population is recorded over a long period. Helgason, for instance, followed a cohort of 5395 born in Iceland in 1895–97 through 60–62 years. From national records he ascertained that nearly 2% (103) of them developed a manic-depressive illness, of whom 34 were dead by 1960, 18 from suicide. Over half of their deaths, therefore, were by suicide and 17% of the manic-depressives in the cohort committed suicide. He also identified 139 neurotic depressives of whom 15 died, but only 1 by suicide, or 7% of the deaths. Similarly, in a more recent survey in which over 3500 residents of Lundby were followed through 25 years it was found that half of the suicides had an endogenous depression.

It is estimated that during a life-time the chance of having a depressive illness severe enough to be referred to a psychiatrist is between 2 and 4%, and that the average lifespan of depressives is 66 years. Assuming further that 15% will die by suicide, then the expected yearly number of suicides in England and Wales occurring in the course of a depressive illness would be between 2250 and 2500. That is, about half the annual 5000 suicides would be suffering in this way, a proportion not only similar to the 64% found in the 100 clinically assessed suicides in Sussex and Hampshire—a sample which closely resembled the national one as regards its age and sex composition—but also to the figure reported when cohorts of depressives are followed over a long period.

Attempted suicide

Research on attempted suicide has also contributed to our understanding of the relation of suicide to depression, and to the kind of action which could forestall suicide. A number of studies have used modern statistical methods to identify the different categories of people who attempt suicide. Each of seven analyses of this kind identified a discrete group of suicide attempts that differed from the others in being made by individuals who were severely or psychotically depressed and who made a serious attempt in circumstances which made discovery unlikely, and in whom the intent to die was apparent. This group who were severely depressed differed in several respects from the larger group, now generally known as cases of parasuicide, who made an apparent suicide attempt involving deliberate self-harm but without the serious intent to die.[2] While the severely depressed group consisted largely of males aged 45 or more, the parasuicide group was made up mainly of younger females including a proportion of adolescents: they were commonly motivated by frustration, anger or despair, and they often chose a setting for the attempt in which intervention was likely.

Other investigators have used a clinical, rather than a statistical, approach to the problem in which the seriousness of the intent to die was rated. The consensus of ten such studies is that the feature most closely associated with the intent to die was, again, a diagnosis of manic-depressive or primary depressive illness and a high score on scales that assess the severity of depression. Pallis, reviewing this work, inferred that patients making a serious attempt resemble those dying by suicide rather than attempted suicides in general. This conclusion is supported by research in which attempted suicides were followed up for a year or more and their outcome assessed in terms of subsequent suicidal acts. When this was done it was found that more patients whose attempts were initially rated as serious subsequently committed suicide than did those whose attempts were rated as less serious.[3]

In one investigation, for example, 151 consecutive cases of suicide attempt admitted to an Emergency Department were clinically assessed. Each of them was scored on the physical seriousness of the attempt (the danger to life incurred by the method used) and on two scales, one of which assessed the patient's intent to die (Beck's scale) and the other, by listing the known characteristics of suicides, enabled the risk of the patient committing suicide to be scored. Intent to die not only correlated closely with both suicide risk and the medical seriousness, but also with the number and severity of the depressive symptoms. Accordingly, it was found that the following features of depressive illness distinguished the high from low intent suicidal acts: insomnia, pessimism, loss of usual interests and social withdrawal, feelings of worthlessness and loss of weight, and such behaviour as slowness of speech and a discouraged posture. In addition, the two groups differed significantly in those demographic and social characteristics which are known to be strongly associated with consummated suicide, namely living alone, being separated or divorced, over 45 and male. So it is evident that the features of a person making a serious suicide attempt closely resemble those found in actual suicides by interviewing their relatives soon after the act. Similarly, using samples of serious and non-serious suicide attempts drawn from a Psychiatric Case Register of patients who had been given a personality test (the MMPI), Pallis and Birtchnell were able to show that the personalities of those who made serious suicide attempts also resembled those who later died by suicide, while the personalities of both these groups differed from the non-serious group. It was also of interest that the predominantly young, female, non-serious attempters had the most seriously disturbed personality profiles.

So far, then, recent research has established that suicides commonly suffer from a primary depression and that attempted suicides in whom the intent to die is serious also have a high incidence of severe depression and high risk of subsequently dying by suicide. Clearly, diagnosing depression is a priority in assessing whether a person is a suicide risk. Nevertheless, the *clinical* similarities between depressed suicides and living depressives are more apparent than the differences. Accordingly, other interacting factors need to be taken into account in order to predict those depressives who are most likely to die by suicide, especially as depression is a common condition.

Other research has indicated what further factors need to be considered. The first of these is the socio-cultural environment. Suicides, for example, tend to be more frequent in the more affluent socio-economic classes and among those who live alone. Secondly, life-stresses and adverse events, notably bereavements in the preceding two years, have been shown to be closely associated with suicide, as also have moving house and loss of employment.[4]

In order to elucidate the interdependence of the various factors—mental illness and personality, social circumstances, and psychosocial stresses—and in order to pursue the hypothesis that the more closely the individual attempting suicide resembles the completed suicide the greater the risk of the person subsequently killing himself, Pallis planned a project which compared his series of attempted suicides and suicides whose relatives were interviewed. Both groups had been interviewed using the same standard questions. A form of statistical analysis was then applied to the combined samples to see whether the responses to 55 of the items would discriminate between the suicides and the attempted suicides. In fact, they were able to allocate 92% of the cases correctly to their respective groups. Among other attributes, the suicides were once again also distinguished by the now familiar clinical manifestations of a manic-depressive illness. On the basis of these discriminating items Pallis next constructed a suicide risk-scale, and the ability of the scale correctly to predict which suicide attempters would later kill themselves was tested by applying the scale to over 700 cases of suicide attempts who had been followed up through three years in Wales. The suicides were identified with a high degree of probability.

Suicide prevention

One practical implication of these studies of suicide is that by developing intent and risk scales it is feasible not only to show that the severely depressed are highly vulnerable to suicide, but to predict with reasonable accuracy whether or not someone who has made a suicide attempt will make a further and fatal attempt. Consequently, these studies have real preventive value in helping doctors in busy

Emergency Departments to assess and decide on the appropriate management of the large numbers of attempted suicides with which they have to deal these days.

In summary, suicide prevention largely depends on the ability of the primary care service (the General Practitioner, Emergency Departments and so on) (a) to recognise the vulnerable depressive and the characteristics of patients that denote a high risk for suicide, (b) to provide effective treatment for depression and (c) to organise efficient aftercare. These claims are supported by studies of the ways in which the suicidally depressed are currently identified and managed.

Barraclough and his colleagues investigated the warnings given by a series of suicides in 1966. Whereas only 19% of the 64 uncomplicated depressives made an unequivocal threat of suicide in the month before death, nearly half of the alcoholic ones did so. Of greater preventive relevance was that over half of the depressives contacted their General Practitioner in the last month. And, surprisingly, a high proportion of depressed suicide attempters were also reported to have seen their doctors just prior to the act. It is apparent that the majority of suicidal depressives offer ample opportunities for intervention, providing the doctor has the skills which enable him to recognise the suicide risk.

It is of interest, next, to see how the GPs managed the suicidal depressives at that time, and hence to what extent prevention is practicable. Eighty-one per cent had been prescribed hypnotics and tranquillisers, so their doctors at least recognised that they were distressed. Nevertheless, in only 1 of the 19 who were given antidepressants was the dosage and type appropriate. Furthermore, over half had been prescribed barbiturates, and half the depressives dying from barbiturates had received the tablets in the previous week, all but 2 using the prescribed tablets to commit suicide. Clearly in 1966 there was scope for more expertise in the primary care of suicidal depressives; but there is reason to believe that since then their recognition and management may have improved with the rapid extension of postgraduate education.

The number of suicides has fallen significantly in England since the 1960s. While seeking explanations for the decline, one of the possibilities entertained was that it could be ascribed to improved mental health services, especially primary care. Jenkins, therefore, compared the consultation rates and diagnoses recorded in two surveys of general practice in England: one in 1955–56 and the other in 1970–71. He found that whereas the consultation rates for *all* conditions fell, those for psychiatric disorder increased by 60%; secondly, the General Practitioners' diagnoses in the more recent period were more in accordance with psychiatric conventions; and thirdly, the number of patients recognised as suffering from disorders with a high suicide risk had greatly increased, especially depressive disorders. It was tentatively inferred that GPs attitudes to the depressive patient are changing in a direction that could help to curtail suicide.

Another factor which has been suggested as a reason for the decline in the suicide rate is the increased activity of voluntary organisations, such as the Samaritans in the UK, which offer help to people who are depressed and which have done much to increase the awareness of the general public of the risk of suicide. A study of the suicide rates in towns with active Samaritan groups showed a significantly lower incidence of suicide in those towns than in other towns without such voluntary groups, and further research could be helpful in clarifying the factors mainly responsible for differences of this kind. Other factors that could play a part in reducing the suicide rate are the reduced prescribing of barbiturate drugs and the reduction in the toxicity of the domestic gas supply.

The practicability of applying the recent advances in the treatment of depression to suicide prevention can be illustrated by considering the potential benefits of lithium clinics which provide the facilities required for administering lithium treatment. Using the criteria of recurrence and the success rate that Coppen and his colleagues reported in a controlled trial of the prophylactic value of lithium in recurrent depression, Barraclough identified 21 recurrent depressives in his sample of suicides who would have qualified for the trial. He then calculated that had these depressives been treated with lithium as successfully as the trial patients, a fifth of the suicides would have been prevented; and extrapolating to the country as a whole there would have been 750 fewer suicides.

The general management of the depressive is equally in need of appraisal: too many depressives in psychiatric treatment still commit suicide. Previous work has already shown that the quickest and surest way of removing the suicidal depressive from danger is still by admission to hospital and giving electroshock treatment (ECT). Despite this, it has been found that suicides not only received less ECT than other depressives and spent less time in hospital, but that they also antagonised the staff more. These problems of management led Pallis to ask general practitioners, psychiatrists, nurses and Samaritans about their knowledge of suicide risks and attitudes to the suicidal. Only the psychiatrists considered a primary responsibility for preventing suicide lay with them and, though most of the respondents knew that depression increases the risk of suicide, they were largely ignorant of other risk factors. Since few of the suicidally depressed contact social and lay services, the key to prevention remains in the hands of the doctors and psychiatrists.

Recently the suicide rates of resident psychiatric patients in England and elsewhere have shown a disturbing increase, and one which coincides with the introduction of more liberal regimes.[5] Whether the present preference for early discharge and for treating depressives in the community places the suicidal patient at greater risk has yet to be decided. Nevertheless, we have sufficient facts to plan preventive management. We know the danger of suicide relates to the onset of a depression and to its duration; it also increases in the weeks following discharge from active treatment. The importance of systematic after-care in the community is evident.

Walk has given other grounds for claiming that a well-organised community psychiatric service might, in fact, be able to reduce the suicide rate. He compared the suicide rates of all patients in contact with a psychiatrist during the five years before and after the introduction of the Chichester Community Psychiatric Service in which 86% of all referrals are treated in the community. He found a significant decrease in the suicide rate of elderly psychiatric patients. Since it was the aged depressed patients who had benefited most, and whose level of referral had increased most after starting community care, it appeared that the new services had been helpful.

To sum up: the facts derived from recent research on the relation of suicide to depression, on the characteristics of the suicidal depressive, and on new opportunities for effective treatment are such that suicide must now be considered at least partially preventable. As a first step the health services should provide more efficient management and after-care for those who are depressed.

References

1. Sainsbury P. (1982). Depression and suicide prevention. *Bibliotheca Psyciatrica*; **162**: 17–32.
2. Dyer J. A. T., Kreitman N. (1984). Hopelessness, depression and suicidal intent in parasuicide. *Brit. J. Psychiat*; **144**: 127–33.
3. Pallis D. J., Gibbons J. S., Pierce D. W. (1984). Estimating suicide risk among attempted suicides. *Brit. J. Psychiat*; **144**: 139–48.
4. Cooke D. J., Hole D. J. (1983). The aetiological importance of stressful life events. *Brit. J. Psychiat*; **143**: 397–400.
5. McClure G. M. G. (1984) Trends in suicide rate in England and Wales 1975–80. *Brit. J. Psychiat*; **144**: 119–26.

6
Causes and Treatment of Depression

Why do people get depressed? Depression is an emotional state we all experience from time to time as a normal reaction to serious disappointments and other forms of frustration. Depression is pathological and a symptom of mental disorder when it is excessive or uncontrolled and when it persists without any reasonable cause.[1] Depressive illness occurring mainly as a result of a specific causal event such as a bereavement is commonly described as 'reactive', while the term 'endogenous' is used for depressive illness arising without a tangible external cause and, therefore, attributable mainly to internal constitutional factors. Attacks of endogenous depression may occur without any warning. Thus a person who has been leading a normal, active life may unexpectedly wake up one morning in a state of deep despair, unable to go to work, feeling that life is not worth living and thinking up ways of ending it.

When we find a patient severely depressed for no apparent reason what constitutional factors could be responsible for the condition? Is there some biochemical abnormality affecting the normal functions of the body, or is there an abnormality in some small centre in the brain? One of the first investigations to lead to positive findings was that of Coppen and Shaw, who studied the distribution of salts in the body and found that in severe endogenous depression the sodium content of the tissue cells is abnormally high, while during recovery it falls. This, as Naylor showed, implies a defect in the sodium transport mechanism which normally pumps the sodium across the cell membrane and out of the cells. It is known that the transport mechanisms of the cell membrane are influenced by hormones secreted by the endocrine glands, and it is significant that depressive illness tends to occur after childbirth and at the menopause, which are times when considerable endocrine changes are taking place. Depression is also a characteristic symptom of Cushing's Disease in which there is abnormal function of the endocrine glands controlled by the hypothalamus in the brain. Taken together with other investigations indicating abnormalities in the release of other hormones (growth hormone and thyroid stimulating hormone) these results strongly suggest that in certain types of depressive illness a defect in the regulatory mechanisms of the hypothalamus is mainly responsible for the condition.

A different approach was made by investigators who tried to obtain information about the functioning of the neurotransmitter amines such as noradrenaline and tryptophan in the brain. As long ago as 1963 Ashcroft demonstrated that many depressed patients have an abnormally low level in their cerebrospinal fluid of a breakdown product of tryptophan (5-HIAA). This finding was confirmed by Van Praag, using different experimental techniques, and also by Åsberg, who noted an association between low concentrations of the tryptophan break-down product and high rates of suicide. Work with laboratory animals had shown that drugs which caused depression reduced the activity of these neurotransmitter amines at their sites of action in the brain. Conversely, drugs which elevate the mood, such as amphetamine ('speed'), cocaine and the antidepressant drugs, all increase the activity of the neurotransmitter amines of the brain. This is also the effect of electroshock treatment (ECT). Findings of this kind have led to the 'neurotransmission amine' theory of depression, which postulates that depression is caused by an imbalance of neurotransmitter amines in certain pathways in the brain. Stemming from this theory, clinicians have estimated the concentrations of amine break-down products in the urine of depressed patients, and three groups of workers have reported reduced levels of a break-down product of noradrenaline (MHPG) in the urine of many of the patients suffering from depression. It is not to be expected that the mechanisms giving rise to depressive illness are the same in every case, but there is considerable evidence that depression is frequently associated with abnormal functioning of the transmitter amines in the brain.

It is a well established observation that endogenous depressive illness tends to run in families. This has been confirmed by the genetic studies of Perris in Sweden, Angst in Switzerland and Winokur in the USA, who have shown that endogenous depressive illnesses can be subdivided into two main types. Briefly, they have shown that patients who have recurrent mood swings with recurrent manic as well as depressive illnesses (bipolar affective disorders) are distinct from patients who have depressions without manic attacks (unipolar depression). The natural history of their illnesses is different and the two conditions each breed true within the families. The bipolar and unipolar types of depressive illness differ also in their sex incidence and in their response to treatment with drugs. The identification of further subgroups of illness continues to be an active subject for research. Winokur has claimed that the unipolar group of endogenous depressions includes a further subgroup of 'primary depression' which occurs in middle age and which has an equal incidence in both sexes. This differs from a subgroup of 'depressive spectrum disorders' occurring mainly in younger women whose male relations often show a tendency to alcoholism and behavioural disorders. He has claimed further that the predisposition to the bipolar type of depressive illness is attributable in some families to a gene associated with the x-chromosome. While the precise mechanisms underlying the different types of depressive illness are still under investigation, the importance of genetic factors in certain types of depression is now well established; and since the genes which are inherited are simply chemical compounds (DNA) leading to the formation in the body of specific chemical products, it is evident that chemical factors must play a part in determining the predisposition to certain types of depressive illness. Clinically a patient's symptoms depend not only on the underlying depressive disorder, but also on the basic character of the patient affected, his upbringing, past life experiences and any physical or psychological events that may be affecting him at the time. It is not easy to identify distinct syndromes in a group of patients who differ so widely in their individual symptoms, and in this situation an advance was made by Roth who applied factorial analysis techniques to defining a specific type of endogenous depression by means of the 'Newcastle Scale', which is now increasingly used in clinical studies. This type of depression, however, covers only a minority of depressive patients, and a number of investigators have recently been using factor and cluster analysis of the symptoms in attempting to clarify the heterogenous group of so-called 'neurotic depressives'.

Electroconvulsive treatment (ECT)

Depressive illness is a potentially lethal condition with a high mortality rate owing to the risk of suicide and effective treatment is, therefore, important.

There have been a number of investigations of the value of electroconvulsive therapy (ECT), which was one of the first effective methods of treating depressive illness and which continues to be widely used. Originally this treatment consisted simply in attaching two electrodes to the patient's scalp and giving a brief electric shock sufficient to produce a convulsion. This was associated with a temporary loss of consciousness and afterwards the patient generally experienced a feeling of relief with a marked diminution of the depressive symptoms. The treatment was repeated two or three times a week until the patient was better. While the treatment was found to be very safe and accidents were rare, some temporary loss of memory was often reported and there might be headaches and some temporary confusion, but very occasionally the convulsions caused fractures. In the late 1940s muscle relaxants and anaesthetics were introduced to reduce the risk of fractures, and the treatment is now generally given in this modified form. Another modification that is commonly used today is the unilateral administration of the electric shock to one hemisphere, and this is reported to reduce the loss of memory: but in any case the memory impairment generally diminishes rapidly when the treatment is finished and it rarely persists for more than three months.

In a trial of 281 seriously depressed patients Greenblatt[2] and his colleagues reported marked improvement in 76% treated by ECT compared with only 46% who had been given a placebo. They found that ECT was significantly more effective than drug treatment with imipramine or phenelzine and acted more quickly: it was particularly effective in patients with manic-depressive and involutional types of depressive illness. Other trials, including one carried out in 1965 in the UK by the Medical Research Council,[3] also showed ECT to be highly effective and superior to drug treatments for many patients including those with severe depression of the endogenous type. A more recent survey made in 1980–81 in the UK with the help of the Royal College of Psychiatrists[4,5] confirmed these findings in general and reported that 97% of clinical consultants who were contacted regarded ECT as a useful treatment in certain cases. Many regarded it as specially useful in the elderly and considered it to be safer than treatment by drugs. Mainly because of adverse publicity some patients are unwilling to have ECT, but there are others, such as those who have recurrent attacks of endogenous depression, who ask for ECT and prefer it to drug treatment since it gets them better more quickly.

According to recent surveys some 20 000 patients are treated annually by ECT in Great Britain and 90 000 in the USA, usage rates of 5·6 and 4·4 per 10 000 population. Yet there is strong opposition in some quarters to treatment by ECT due partly to ill-informed criticism in the press and partly to the activities of certain organisations such as the Church of Scientology in the USA. In 1982, after picketing by scientologists of a hospital where ECT was used in

Berkeley, California, an ordinance was passed banning the use of ECT in that city as a misdemeanour, punishable by a fine of $500 or six months imprisonment or both. However in 1983 when a case was tried in court the ordinance banning the use of ECT was rejected by the Judge. This illustrates the need for further education of the public to ensure that the true facts based on careful investigation are more widely known and the public is not misled.

Drug treatments

The introduction of the antidepressive drugs for the treatment of depression was a major advance in this field. As with some other medical advances, their discovery involved an element of chance, but before these drugs could become available for the practical treatment of patients a great deal of basic laboratory and clinical research had to be carried out. The introduction of *iproniazid*, an inhibitor of the enzyme monoamine oxidase, followed laboratory work in the USA by Udenfriend and Brodie, who found that iproniazid reversed the depressant action of the drug reserpine in animal experiments, producing behavioural excitement. This they attributed to its action in increasing the level of neurotransmitter amines in the brain. These pharmacological findings encouraged some psychiatrists to try treating depressed patients with reserpine and iproniazid. It was only later that the use of reserpine was found to be unnecessary, since iproniazid was effective alone in increasing the concentration of neurotransmitter amines in the brain and so relieving the depression in patients with depressive illness.

Another drug, *imipramine*, a 'tricyclic' antidepressant, generally behaved as a sedative when tested on animals and it was first used in human patients as a treatment for schizophrenia. It was only as a result of the keen clinical observation of Kuhn that its antidepressant properties were noted. In fact, the basic scientists had no inkling that imipramine might be an antidepressant and it was only the information fed to them by the clinicians which led to their looking again for antidepressant properties in the laboratory. It was then that the ability of an astute research worker to make use of a laboratory error led to the beginning of our understanding of its mechanism of action. One of the technicians in Brodie's laboratory mistakenly sent up rats belonging to someone else, which had been treated with imipramine for some days. Brodie administered reserpine and was surprised to find a reversal of the usual reserpine sedation effect—instead of being depressed, the rats became excited and overactive. He was astute enough to realise the significance of the mistake, and later the Nobel prize winner Axelrod and his colleagues showed that imipramine increased the level of free neurotransmitter amines in the brain by slowing down their re-uptake into their inactive storage sites.

These observations illustrate a point of some importance, which is the need for close cooperation in research between the basic scientists working in the laboratory and the clinicians who are actively engaged in clinical treatment. As our understanding increases of the neurotransmitter mechanisms operating in the brain, so the pharmacologists are developing new drugs to modify these mechanisms in ways that can be helpful in the treatment of patients. But before any new drug can be brought into general clinical use, an immense amount of work is required in laboratory investigations to determine their safety and to identify possible side effects or unwanted interactions that might limit their application. In the clinical investigations of new drugs, it is a basic rule that the patient's interests must always come first. It is, therefore, essential that any investigation that is proposed must be fully explained to the patient and his agreement obtained in writing. To safeguard any patients who do not fully understand the implications of research, agreement must also be obtained from the hospital Ethical Committee.

Mental illnesses tend to fluctuate in the severity of the symptoms, both spontaneously and because of environmental events, and improvement or other incidental changes in a patient's condition might, therefore, be wrongly attributed to the treatment being given at the time.

A new drug can be tested against an inert substance, or 'placebo', but in the case of depressive illness we now have drugs of known therapeutic action and any new antidepressant drug can, therefore, be tested against one of these standard drugs. The patients can be divided randomly into two or more identical groups of sufficient size to obviate, by the law of averages, any differences between the groups due to environmental or other effects. The only difference is that the one group is given the trial drug and the other a placebo or a standard remedy. In a 'double blind' controlled trial all the preparations are made up in identical form so that neither the patient nor the doctor who carries out their assessment knows which preparation a patient is receiving, and he cannot therefore be influenced by preconceived ideas. At the end of the trial the results of the treatment are analysed statistically to see which drug treatment is most beneficial. This method has proved immensely useful in identifying drugs that are of real value and those which are relatively ineffective and which might otherwise remain on the market and prevent improvement in treatment, perhaps for many years.

The antidepressant drugs have brought tremendous benefit to depressed patients and have greatly reduced the need for ECT. Of equal moment has been the discovery of the benefit of treatment with lithium.[6] In the old days many manic-depressive patients had to be hospitalised several times a year for years on end. For these patients with frequent mood swings between mania and depression lithium treatment can literally transform their lives. Cade has the credit for introducing lithium as a treatment for mania, and its usefulness in this condition has now been amply confirmed. The more important use of lithium as a prophylactic in preventing relapses in manic-depressive illnesses was noted by Maggs and established in extensive trials by Mogens Schou in Denmark. In manic-depressive disorders with frequent relapses up to 70% of patients treated with lithium have a marked or complete reduction in the frequency and severity of their attacks.

A patient's response to treatment depends partly on the type of depressive illness from which he is suffering. While those with bipolar depression respond well to lithium, patients with unipolar depression are generally found to respond best to the tricyclic antidepressants. The response to treatment also depends partly on factors in the patient's genetic make-up which determine the blood level of the drug that is reached after administration of a standard dose. It was shown by Hammer that there are large individual differences in the blood levels in patients receiving standard doses of antidepressants and, besides the influence of the genetic make-up, the blood levels that are reached are affected also by factors such as the intake of alcohol or other drugs. An important part of the treatment of many patients with depressive illness is, therefore, to have available the laboratory facilities that are required for carrying out the regular estimation of the levels of lithium or antidepressants in the blood.

Clearly there are many problems still remaining to be solved, but basic and clinical research have added greatly to our understanding of the factors involved in the causation of depressive illness and have resulted in a big improvement in the methods available for treatment. What was formerly regarded as an incurable condition requiring permanent hospital care is now generally accepted as an eminently treatable form of mental disorder. The saving in terms of human suffering, as well as in cost to the community, has been immense.

References

1. Storr A. (1983). A psychotherapist looks at depression. *Brit. J. Psychiat*; **143**: 431–5.
2. Greenblatt M., Grosser G. H., Wechsler H. (1964). Differential response of hospitalised depressed patients to somatic therapy. *Amer. J. Psychiat*; **120**: 231–9.
3. Medical Research Council (1965). Report by Clinical Psychiatry Committee. Clinical trial of the treatment of depressive illness. *Brit. Med. J*; **1**: 881–6.
4. Pippard J., Ellam L. (1981). *Electroconvulsive Treatment in Great Britain, 1980*. London: Royal College of Psychiatrists.

5. Clinical Research Centre, Division of Psychiatry (1984). The Northwick Park ECT trial. Predictors of response to real and simulated ECT. *Brit. J. Psychiat*; **144**: 227–37.
6. Abou-Saleh M. T., Coppen A. (1983). Classification of depression and response to antidepressive therapies. *Brit. J. Psychiat*; **143**: 601–3.

7
New Clinical and Laboratory Techniques

Today's problems are sometimes illuminated by those of the past. In the Croonian Lectures delivered in 1849 at the Royal College of Physicians in London Dr John Conolly, Physician to the Middlesex Lunatic Asylum at Hanwell, devoted two lectures to a disease which was formerly not uncommon, but which has become rare today as a result of research—*general paralysis of the insane* (GPI). This illness usually begins with some change of character in the sufferer, a loss of judgement and of ethical standards, a loss of drive and grasp, a slowing of thought, cooling of the emotions (sometimes with depression) and a shrinkage of memory. Later there begin to be physical signs of impaired movement—walking is disturbed, the hands become feeble, the bodily dysfunction grows and eventually after a few years the patient dies. Here are some of Dr Conolly's case descriptions:

> 'My own largest and most constant experience is among the insane poor; but yet, in every year, I see some among the noble and the rich, fine active men in the prime of life, whose conduct has become gradually eccentric, whose manner has become more haughty, who have grown more contradictory and irritable, and who have bought horses, or betted beyond their usual custom, or been guilty of some remarkable extravagance; taking wine also more freely, and in some respects losing the habitual reserve or dignity of their character . . .

Within the last two years, among many cases, I remember two particular instances in members of the legal profession. One was a barrister, not yet forty, and who, by toil and talent and high character, had just surmounted the first difficulties of his career as a junior. He would sit all the day with a book or papers before him, writing nothing, reading nothing, doing nothing; but he imagined that he had written and published many volumes of poetry. His appearance, to any stranger entering the room, indicated little want of consciousness; he was calm and gentlemanly in his demeanour, but his speech had the fatal faltering; he walked first with eagerness, and soon staggeringly, and his mental weakness steadily proceeded . . .

The other case was that of a country solicitor, from my native county of Lincoln, about fifty years of age, temperate, moral, exemplary in conduct, and looking hale and healthy. He had been engaged habitually in his professional labours from five or six o'clock in the morning to ten at night. At fifty he broke down. He became grandiloquent; he considered his wealth to be very great; wrote his surgeon a cheque for £1,000; declared himself Duke of Lincolnshire, and at the same time sheriff of Dover, in right of his wife, who, he said, was queen of the queen's bedchamber . . .'

Conolly's asylum had about 800 patients, of whom up to 30 at any one time had this fatal illness. He notes that it was five or six times commoner in men than women, but whereas the men came from all walks of life, the women were exclusively poor, and he never saw a female case from the middle or upper classes. He lists the supposed causes of the illness—bereavement in some, overwork in others, anxieties, domestic unhappiness, and in a few cases immoderate drinking. 'Men of active and well-exercised minds,' he tells us, 'are more disposed to this than to any other form of mental malady.'

In spite of psychological study, the careful description of minute details of the patients and its study postmortem, its cause remained unknown to the 19th century physicians.

Today this disease has almost vanished from our hospitals and from the community.

How has this come about? Pasteur and Koch, among others, showed that some illnesses are caused by organisms such as bacteria which can be taken from the body and grown in the laboratory. These can then be examined through the microscope, stained with special dyes, and inoculated into experimental animals to reproduce the disease. In the last quarter of the 19th century, there was an explosion of new knowledge, with the growth of the new technology of bacteriology. While the different types of microbes were discovered and described, another approach was to investigate the ways in which animal and human bodies reacted to their invasions. In particular, microbes were found to stimulate the formation in the patient of various kinds of antibodies. These are proteins, usually found in the blood, which react specifically with this or that organism, in some cases forming a visible precipitate, in others altering the ease with which the red cells of the blood split and liberate their red colouring. The most significant finding from this new science of immunology was that antibodies, once provoked, continue to exist long after the signs of infection have vanished. By measuring the amounts of antibodies in blood samples from a patient one could, therefore, learn about the patient's past history of infection, and also detect hidden infection still present but not provoking recognisable symptoms.

The mental illness general paralysis (GPI) proved to be due to such an infection, but one contracted as long as ten or twenty years before the appearance of mental symptoms. The original infection was, therefore, long forgotten, if it was even noticed at the time. Syphilis was shown in 1905 by Schaudinn and Hoffmann to be due to infection with a microscopic single-celled organism, a spirochaete and not a bacillus, which may provoke a small temporary ulcer at the point where it enters the body. But it also provokes blood changes, and Wasserman in 1906 announced the form of blood test which enables us to detect occult syphilitic infections. It was the application of this test to asylum patients which gave the first clue to the cause of their trouble, but it was only in 1913 that Noguchi and Moore first demonstrated the spirochaetes of syphilis in brain tissue from people who had died of the disease. These organisms had been dormant for years before they began to interfere with mental function.

Spirochaetes are difficult to kill in the body, but high doses of penicillin have been found to be most effective, and there is no longer any reason why the illness cannot be stopped as soon as it has been diagnosed with the help of the Wasserman reaction. This blood test, which requires a laboratory and a technician, is an essential aid to the diagnosis today. Without its invention the connection between a venereal infection caught at 20 and a mental illness appearing at 40 might never have been made. Without thirty years of solid technical achievement in bacteriology to build upon, the delicate technology for studying a protozoal infection would not have existed. It was impossible for Conolly and his medical colleagues to solve the problem of general paralysis because in their day the necessary scientific knowledge and laboratory equipment were still to come.

Temporal lobe epilepsy

Let us come forward just over a hundred years and look at a couple of cases of another type of mental illness. The first, reported in the *Lancet* in 1954 was of a man, then aged 38, who all his life from early childhood had enjoyed what he called 'thought satisfaction' whenever he looked at a nice bright shiny safety pin. From time to time he used to retire to the lavatory to enjoy this pleasure, which he later described as better than sexual intercourse. It was, in fact, akin to a sexual feeling, the desire to look at pins being aroused by erotic experience or by anxiety. His wife, who saw him indulging, described how he would stare at a pin fixedly for about a minute, become glassy-eyed, make a brief humming noise and suck his lips, and then be unresponsive for about two minutes. A few years later she noticed that his performance had added features: it continued with him marking time with his feet like a sentry and marching backwards briefly, while his right hand plucked at his left sleeve, and then he would recover to normality. During these attacks he never fell, never wet himself, never went blue, and never jerked about in the way that people do in a major epileptic fit. He told the doctor that he had become impotent with his wife and had begun sometimes to dress in her clothes. He also revealed that a real safety pin was not essential—he could get satisfaction simply from dreams or fantasies of pins.

The working and the crude anatomy of his brain were investigated by means of the electroencephalograph (EEG). By attaching wires to various points on the scalp and amplifying the tiny electrical changes they pick up from second to second, it is possible to detect something of what is going on electrically in the parts of the brain inside the skull beneath the wires.[1] Each region has its normal pattern of electrical fluctuations in terms of frequencies and magnitude. In contrast, an abnormal record may be one with violent fluctuations crowding on one another like the seismogram of an earthquake, and this may be associated with strange alterations of consciousness or even a frank epileptic fit. The EEG not only detects such abnormalities, but enables them to be located. X-rays of the head, taken in a special way, can also show a particular zone of brain distortion. In this man these techniques showed that the display of safety pins provoked in him a brief state of altered consciousness and abnormal electrical discharges of epileptiform type. They showed that there was an abnormality of the temporal lobe on the left side of his brain. This provided the surgeon with enough information to open his skull on that side, to see that the left temporal lobe was, in fact, scarred at its front end and to cut out several centimetres of diseased tissue.

He was reviewed 16 months later. From the time of operation he had no further desire to look at safety pins, nor had any more episodes of the type he had hitherto experienced. His sexual potency had come back, he was getting on better with his wife and with his work. In medical terms he had suffered from *temporal lobe epilepsy with fetishism* for nearly 40 years, but had been cured by the brain operation.

Radiology was born in 1895, electroencephalography only in the thirties of the 20th century. Without the availability of these routine diagnostic aids to the hospital physician, and the previous research to discover how best to use them, this patient could not have been successfully treated. The EEG, in particular, has done a great deal to widen our understanding of epilepsy. The episodic 'falling sickness,' with loss of consciousness and convulsions, has been known from ancient times. The EEG has shown that there are many different kinds of epilepsy, some of which show only as brief periods of altered consciousness or of automatic behaviour, without any falling or convulsing, while others develop later into cases showing the symptoms of schizophrenia.[2]

This man's illness had many interesting features. One worth specially noting is the intertwining of the physical and the psychological symptoms. His sexual perversion (the safety pin as fetish) must have had its origins in early childhood learning (à la Freud) which took place at some time after his temporal lobe had been damaged, perhaps by the whooping cough virus. Epilepsy and sexual satisfaction had become linked, and then imagination sufficed to fire the whole experience. Yet the treatment was surgical, not psychoanalytical, in this case.

The second case of this condition, described in the journal *Brain* (1956, 1957), was a woman of 41, a professional singer from a family of epileptics, who herself suffered from fits frequently, but irregularly, from the age of 15. She illustrates in greater detail the possible complexity of the epileptic experience, and how what we call physical or know as mental can seem a continuum. Her fits always followed the same sequence.

She said that when well, she would suddenly begin to feel remote, as if not in her own skin, and she would know a fit was going to come. She would become very active, working at breakneck speed for 10 or 20 minutes, although time seemed to go unnaturally slowly. She would feel more and more remote, as if she were God looking down on the world, yet continue to read, write, sing, know all that was going on, and to fight against the approaching doom; others would be unaware she felt like this. Then would come what she called her halfway point. Suddenly her remoteness increased vastly, and she no longer cared or fought it. She could still talk, but now her voice was altered. She would get a funny idea that she was going to smell something any moment. She would begin to prepare for her fall, that she knew was coming, perhaps in 30 minutes. Suddenly a disgustingly sweet cheap perfume would burst on her. She would stay still and quiet, resting after it had gone away, and then she would start to hear someone away on her right calling her name insistently. She knew she must not look towards them, and tried to resist, but always to no avail, and as she turned her head the major fit broke over her and she lost consciousness altogether.

Her doctor discovered by experimentation that if she sniffed certain strong, unpleasant odours just before her halfway point the epileptic episode would halt in its tracks. Only very few smells would do this. Pure jasmine was one such smell for her, and if she carried a small bottle she could control her epilepsy in good time.

A further step in her treatment made use of the knowledge of conditional reflexes developed by Pavlov in his experiments on dogs. The dog's mouth waters when he sees the food. If you ring a bell each time just before showing the food, in a little while the dog's mouth begins to water simply when the bell is rung. In the same way, as this woman's epileptic attack got under way she looked at a silver bracelet before she sniffed her jasmine and halted her fit. In a little while looking at the bracelet alone would do the trick—although it would evoke a vivid olfactory hallucination of jasmine at the same time. Finally, it was found that a real silver bracelet was unnecessary: the fit would stop simply if, before she reached her halfway point, she thought about the bracelet. This therapeutic success, of course, depended in the first instance on her doctor having had sufficient time to think about the problem and to make experiments. His work was possible only because of the great growth of knowledge of epilepsy in its different manifestations, helped by the EEG, and the application of Pavlovian psychology learned in the laboratory since the start of the twentieth century.[3]

Metabolic defects

Finally, also from the 1950s, here is the case of a boy aged 10½ where biochemistry provided the key to causation and treatment, while other sciences—antibiotics, surgery or experimental psychology, immunology or electroencephalography—were all irrelevant. He was admitted to hospital after a few days of great agitation and restlessness, with frequent crying spells and inability to sleep at night. He said there was an object in his body, that his head was empty and he couldn't think properly. He was afraid of being poisoned. He blamed his mother and his brother and said they did not like him. As an inpatient he was mostly quiet, slow, bewildered and spoke about a finger with yellow stuff on the tip which he said touched his leg in the night, entered his stomach and was burning him inside. He suddenly became terrified, shouting 'Look out, it's there in the bed, it's the finger'.

He was the youngest of four children where the father, a man of unstable personality, had deserted and the mother, a woman of poor intelligence and with little money, was having a difficult time keeping the family together. In fact, at age 7 he had had to go into an institution for six months, and had returned a shy, inhibited, anxious little boy. He changed schools a number of times. He was a finicky eater, and would not touch fresh meat or fish or green vegetables. Some months before he had suffered from an attack of dermatitis, a reddening of the skin rather like sunburn over his face, the back of his neck, his knees and the backs of his hands and wrists, but it had cleared up after three months. Now it seemed to be coming back again.

The skin rash had the appearance of pellagra, a disease which used to be endemic among the poor of southern Italy and the United States before it was learned that it was due to nutritional deficiency, primarily a lack of vitamin B_2, now called nicotinamide. This vitamin is made by the body from the amino-acid tryptophan, a component of all animal and some vegetable proteins, and an essential chemical of the diet. However, man cannot make enough to satisfy his total daily requirement of the vitamin and he must get some of it preformed in his food, where it is quite widely available. Lack of nicotinamide leads eventually to skin disease and mental symptoms, the disorder known as pellagra.

This boy, in spite of his finicky eating, was on a nutritionally adequate diet, with about 12 mg nicotinamide per day. In spite of his adequate diet, it was decided to give him extra nicotinamide, and within 48 hours he was very much better, and never looked back. Why did he need so much nicotinamide?

Further study showed that his body suffered from a generalised defect of a special kind. Tryptophan produced during digestion was allowed to leak out in the urine, so that it was, therefore, not available within the body to be converted into nicotinamide. This doubled the daily requirement of preformed nicotinamide from the food.

Such an abnormality is rare, but it can be detected by urine tests. Surveys have found other individuals with the same biochemical deficit, but without any skin trouble, and often without any mental disturbance, presumably because they were getting enough nicotinamide in their diet. One study of 54 cases noted that anxiety, depression and hallucinations occurred in only 14 of them but 3 of them were seen first by the psychiatrist before the chemistry was done. Thus the investigation of the case of the boy led on to the recognition of adult cases, and to understanding mental illnesses which might have been impossible to solve and treat, but for the knowledge developed from experience with him. This knowledge, in turn, has been won through the application of biochemical techniques.

This defect in the chemical machinery of the body is one example of a considerable number of other abnormalities now known, all rare, all genetically determined, and most of them producing mental defect rather than mental illness. The best known of the defects, which partially prevents normal growth of the brain during infancy and childhood, is phenylketonuria, an inability to make use of another normal dietary component, the amino-acid phenylalanine. Here the knowledge won has proved useful in prevention. A baby so afflicted, if detected in time by a urine test, can be brought up on a special diet almost devoid of phenylalanine, and it will then develop normally.

Such successes depend upon technology at a variety of different levels. A chemical industry which can make nicotinamide or remove the phenylalanine from foods is one factor; the invention of paper chromatography—a simple technique for examining large numbers of urine and blood specimens to discover chemical abnormalities—is another; the availability of research laboratories close to the original patients is a third. To make these steps forward, the doctor must have time to think, and time to read about the progress of sciences which may have a bearing on the patient's symptoms. He must also be in close touch with laboratory specialists who can apply their expertise in the individual case. This has been a major handicap so far in understanding mental illness, for the value of laboratories, scientific machines and scientists has been understood in general medicine, but not in psychological medicine until very recently, and their provision still lags.

The causes of mental disorder

Words can mislead, assumptions betray. Psychological symptoms and mental illnesses are so named because their most evident manifestations are in the realms of feeling, thinking and behaving. But that is not to say that all such manifestations are purely mental, or that all causes must be psychological. Of course, the person we are today has been shaped by childhood experiences, by the growth of habits, by relationships with parents and others; and we are responsive to education, psychotherapy, and a variety of human influences. But equally our personality and mental functioning are at the mercy of our genetic equipment, our ductless glands, the intact structure of the brain, and what we take chemically into our body.[4] The baby born without sufficient thyroid gland becomes a cretin, the youth who bangs his head in a motor crash undergoes a personality change, the heavy drinker may with alcohol ease his pain and dull his wits and sometimes end up in madness. Consciousness and voluntary behaviour are not separate from brain and body, they are for medicine different aspects of the human unity. There are many intertwining causes which explain what we are today, and we pick out as most important the one we think we can do something about. The safety pin fetishist must have learned this satisfaction in childhood, and perhaps analytical psychotherapy might have improved him: but in his case surgery was simpler. The general paralytic had an infection treated with penicillin, yet he probably caught syphilis through a voluntary act, as the sort of person he then was. And why did he have a mental illness anyway? Not all syphilitic infections progress beyond the first stage; of those that do, not all attack the brain; why was this sufferer selected? On the other hand, even something as mechanical and unwilled as an epileptic fit, with its electric storm in the brain, can be arrested by a suitable concentrated thought, as the singer showed with her silver bracelet.

The psychiatrist's job is to solve behavioural problems, particularly those which in some way prevent the individual from enjoying normal relationships with other people—whether these are sexual, social or in work. The child who refuses to go to school and clings to mother may be helped to normal confidence and life by family therapy—discussion with all members of the family together to increase understanding and modify handling. The man with a brain damaged in a car crash may need understanding and gentle handling to bring him back to home and work. The girl with a phobia of spiders, or of open spaces (agoraphobia) which keeps her house-bound can be cured by the techniques of behaviour therapy. These are psychological methods, and knowledge of biochemistry or immunology or electroencephalography is irrelevant to these cases. In other patients it may be best to suppress their sleeplessness or unpleasant anxiety by means of a hypnotic, or to modify their unnatural gloom and inability to cope with life by electroconvulsive treatment, or to clarify their bad thinking with a phenothiazine. One method does not exclude another: all which are effective are good.

The brain even to the naked eye is an organ of complex and mysterious structure, and there is about a kilo-and-a-half of it in each of us. It receives a stream of impressions from the world without, and combines them with a selective flow from memory stores. It issues a sequence of acts which is coherent and purposeful. It seems clear that the therapist can influence the outflow of acts either by feeding in new impressions and adding new memories, or by interfering physically with the internal connections. In psychiatric treatment both approaches may be used at once. By the same token, in investigating a psychiatric case the doctor needs to be sure which mental functions are altered and also which aspects of brain structure and working—if any—are abnormal, so that all kinds of medical techniques may be used. As far as the causes of mental illness are concerned it is already very clear that there are many different causes which can produce the same behavioural end result. One of the doctor's jobs is to decide which cause is important in a particular individual patient, because the treatment, to be successful, must be individualised.

People sometimes ask whether science will discover the cause of schizophrenia. This is a misunderstanding on at least two counts. There will not be only one cause—several are indeed already known that have been 'discovered by science'. Temporal lobe epilepsy, the consequence of abnormal brain tissue, sometimes turns into a schizophrenic illness. Drug abusers who chronically take large doses of amphetamines may develop schizophrenic illnesses (which disappear when the drug poisoning is cleared up). In some people a genetic predisposition to schizophrenia can be demonstrated. In others there is a strong suspicion that schizophrenia is a late result of a virus infection. In yet others we have no firm idea why the illness has developed. The treatment of schizophrenia is at present not based on causes, but on the discovery of drugs—phenothiazines and butyrophenones—which can abolish some or all of the symptoms in some cases. This only partial therapeutic success is a challenge to research: is it something about the drug (e.g. wrong dose?) or something about the patient (e.g. particular cause?) when the symptoms fail to respond? The very first of these drugs is less than 30 years old, not a long time to learn all about it.

A person may live seventy years or more and have a variety of illnesses in that lifetime. Psychological or mental illness is one which may appear at any time from young childhood to old age, and which usually disappears again after a while, but may recur. Is an illness at 60 connected with an illness at 6? One way to study this is to keep medical records over a lifetime and see what has happened in different individuals, making comparisons within and between populations. The computer, which so easily stores and associates a multitude of facts has become an important tool in this sort of research.

Technological advances

The deep-freeze has made possible the preservation of the brains of patients who have died, so that their detailed anatomy and chemistry can be analysed at leisure and related to the diseases suffered during life. The telephone, the car and the plane enable an organisation to be mounted whereby the brains of people with particular illnesses can be gathered from a wide area soon after death and brought quickly to the specialised laboratory, where the electron microscope can examine a single nerve cell and a spectrophotometer or liquid scintillation counter can measure the metabolic activities of a few cells from some anatomical region.

But it is investigation of the living brain which is most important to the doctor. A plain x-ray of the head will show details of the bony skull and any calcified points, perhaps along a blood vessel, within the brain itself. But brain tissue is too soft and watery to show up clearly. We can improve matters by withdrawing fluid from the hollow centre of the brain and substituting air, but still what we get is a kind of shadowgraph of the whole brain at once, one bit superimposed on another. Recently *computerised axial tomography* (CAT scanning) has been invented in the UK and it promises to be a major step forward.[5] In tomography by means of rapid automatic focussing and refocussing the details of structure at any desired cross-section of the brain can be scanned by x-ray, the rest of the organ being kept out of focus. By linking the scanner to amplifiers and computer we can increase the sensitivity and make possible the display of living brain anatomy on a screen, selecting areas of particular interest. This has already begun to alter psychiatric practice in several ways. Surveys have shown that some chronic alcoholics (and also some chronic schizophrenics) have shrunken brains, previously unsuspected, and these subgroups of patients will clearly need somewhat different treatment from those whose brains remain normal in size. In a wide range of other people considerable loss of brain substance is now being detected unexpectedly from time to time. It seems likely that only certain parts of the brain are specially important for behavioural abnormality, and one can lose large amounts of other areas without it seeming to affect behaviour. This is a new step forward towards the individualisation of diagnosis and of treatment.

The computer finds quite a different application in aiding the psychologist in giving intelligence tests or testing reaction times repeatedly in a patient. Many of the tests in standard use can be presented on a screen in a standard way; the testee responds by punching particular keys like a typewriter while the machine records the results, compares them with norms and previous tests and prints out the statistically-analysed results. This is a very new technique and its worth in the treatment of patients is still to be fully evaluated. It could be a valuable diagnostic screen and an objective way of assessing the progress of treatment, because it enables many more tests to be done per week and the tests to be more frequently repeated on the same person than is possible with a human interviewer with paper and pencil.

The growing ability to measure something quickly and repeatedly, and in the hands of a junior technician rather than a PhD, is transforming human biochemistry in its application to diagnosis, drug treatment, and research aimed at increasing our understanding of the way the brain works. Hormones and drugs often occur in the blood in very small quantities. A new way of measuring how much is present in a very small blood sample (so that frequent re-sampling does not bleed the patient unduly and produce anaemia), is by the technique known as *radio-immuno-assay*.[6]

Since radioactivity measures are extremely sensitive and highly automated, and immunological reactions can be run on extremely small quantities of patients' blood, techniques of this type are rapidly increasing. They can be applied to measure the amount of drug actually reaching the brain or even being bound to a particular part of it in a patient during treatment, quantities which may bear little relation to the doses of tablets being taken, but which may determine the success of treatment. They can be applied to measure the amount of a particular hormone circulating in a patient's blood every 5 to 10 minutes.[7] Since this is under direct brain control, changes in the amount of hormone may indicate changes in the working of some definite part of the brain, whether as a consequence of stress or of disease. This approach, still in its infancy, promises to expand our knowledge of human brain function in mental illness in quite new ways.

References

1. Fenton G. (1980). Priorities in research related to neuropsychiatry. In *Priorities in Psychiatric Research*. (Lader M., ed) pp. 163–92. Chichester: John Wiley & Sons.
2. Sylvester P. E. (1984). Ammon's horn or hippocampal sclerosis without epilepsy in mental handicap. *Brit. J. Psychiat*; **144**: 538–41.
3. McHugh P. R., Robinson R. G. (1983). The two-way trade — psychiatry and neuroscience. *Brit. J. Psychiat*; **143**: 303–5.
4. Lipowski Z. J. (1984). Organic mental disorders—an American perspective. *Brit. J. Psychiat*; **144**: 542–6.

5. Huckman M. S., Fox J. H., Topel J. L. (1975). Criteria for the diagnosis of cortical atrophy by computerised tomography. *Radiology;* **116**: 85–92.
6. Wiles D. H., Franklin M. (1978). Radioimmunoassay for fluphenazine in human plasma. *Brit. J. Clin. Pharmacol;* **5**: 265–8.
7. Swartz C., Abrams R. (1984). Prolactin levels after bilateral and unilateral ECT. *Brit. J. Psychiat;* **144**: 643–5.

8
Social Influences in Schizophrenia

The nature of schizophrenia

Many years ago the English psychiatrist John Haslam and the French psychiatrist Phillip Pinel recognised syndromes which came on in early adult life, characterised by a change of personality, with symptoms such as thought disorder, delusions, hallucinations and inappropriate emotional reaction, generally leading progressively to mental deterioration. Cases with episodes of extreme inertia or stupor were described as 'catatonic' and those with systematised delusions were called 'paranoid', while cases characterised mainly by silly mannerisms and senseless laughter were known as 'hebephrenic'. Emil Kraepelin noted that many of these illnesses have a poor long-term outcome, and he gave the name 'dementia praecox' to the syndromes characterised by this feature which distinguished them from the illnesses of manic-depressive type which are generally followed by a return to normality. While dementia praecox may start with recurrent episodes of illness, these are never followed by a complete return to normality, so that there is always a progressive deterioration of the personality. The investigations of dementia praecox carried out by Eugen Bleuler led him to conclude that it is not a single homogeneous condition, but made up of a number of related forms of illness, and that it is better to define a somewhat larger group of illnesses with common psychological features which he called the 'group of schizophrenias' (schizophrenia meaning 'split mind'). The features he saw as characteristic of this group were an abnormal loosening of the associations between ideas, a tendency for two opposing thoughts, wishes or emotions to be present in the mind at the same time (ambivalence), withdrawal from reality (autism) and inability to make an appropriate emotional response.

Bleuler regarded the psychological symptoms he had described as being present in every case of schizophrenia, but it was found that these symptoms cannot be clearly defined so that independent observers will always agree on their presence in an individual patient. A diagnosis based on these symptoms could therefore be in doubt. A different approach was made by Kurt Schneider who suggested that there are certain 'first rank' symptoms which, when present in the absence of organic brain disease, invariably indicate that the illness is a schizophrenic one. The symptoms Schneider considered characteristic included delusions of control, as for example the conviction that thoughts are put into or removed from one's head, or that one's actions or feelings are controlled by some external force. Other symptoms he considered characteristic were auditory hallucinations such as hearing voices talking about one in the third person or hearing one's thoughts spoken aloud. Schneider's first rank symptoms have the merit that they can be reliably assessed, so that they can be used to define a particular group of schizophrenic illnesses, but there are also many types of mental illness which according to current usage are described as schizophrenic, but in which the symptoms are not of Schneider's first rank type. It has also become clear that these first rank symptoms are not a good predictor of poor long-term outcome, so that the group of schizophrenic illnesses defined in Schneider's terms differs to some extent from the dementia praecox group with poor long-term outcome previously described by Kraepelin.

The present position is that schizophrenia is currently recognised as a term applied to a group of similar, but by no means identical, mental illnesses. There are many different varieties of schizophrenia and what is included in the group depends on the precise definition that is used. Further research might be helpful in defining more clearly particular subgroups of schizophrenic illness.

Social influences on the course of schizophrenia

The part played by social factors in the causation and maintenance of schizophrenia has been investigated in several large scale population studies. Since there is no laboratory test for schizophrenia, the diagnosis must rest entirely on the pattern of symptoms and signs and the history of their development in the individual patient. In the International Pilot Study of Schizophrenia (IPSS) conducted by the World Health Organization effective use was made of the standardised clinical assessment of the Present State Examination (PSE). This involves the administration of a standard list of specific questions to which the answers are rated on a numerical scale. Each item on the questionnaire, relating either to a symptom or a sign, has an extensive definition attached to it. The interviewer is trained to know this definition thoroughly and to appreciate the way in which it separates a particular item from others with which it might be confused. During the interview it is his task to determine whether the experiences the patient is reporting match up to the definitions he has learned.

A further advantage of the PSE is that a computer programme, named Catego, has been developed to process the interviewers' ratings and to provide a diagnosis. Thus, not only are the observations of signs and symptoms standardised, but also the process of decision-making that leads to a diagnosis. Of course, the Catego programme has no absolute validity. It represents the diagnostic rules of one psychiatrist, but these can then be examined and compared with the rules embodied in programmes constructed by other psychiatrists. The development of standardised clinical interviews linked to diagnostic computer programmes represents a major methodological achievement in psychiatry, which, for the first time allows comparison of research findings in different centres within one country, and across different countries.

One aim of the IPSS investigation was to determine whether psychiatrists in a wide variety of cultures used the term schizophrenia for the same kind of illness. The countries involved were Colombia, Czechoslovakia, Denmark, Formosa, India, Nigeria, the UK, the US and the USSR. Psychiatrists from centres in each country were trained to use the PSE in the same way, and they then interviewed a sample of psychotic patients in their own language. This required translation of the PSE from English into seven other languages including Chinese and Yoruba, a Nigerian tongue. In general few difficulties were encountered in this process, which was completed successfully. About one hundred patients, most of them admitted to hospital, were interviewed in each of the nine centres, and the PSE material of those given the same diagnosis was compared. The Catego programme was applied to the PSE data and yielded a set of standardised diagnoses which acted as a yardstick, against which the diagnoses made by the centre psychiatrists could be set. It was found that in seven of the nine centres agreement between a centre diagnosis of schizophrenia and Catego diagnosis was very high, amounting to 96%. In two centres, those in Washington and in Moscow, agreement was considerably lower, at 71%, and it was evident that the psychiatrists involved were using much broader definitions of schizophrenia than in the other seven centres. The general conclusion of the study, however, was encouraging in that the concept of schizophrenia was shown to be stable across vast cultural chasms; for example, between an African villager and a dweller in a European suburb. This result provided a solid basis for research into schizophrenia as an illness defined in terms of signs and symptoms, even in the absence of confirmatory laboratory tests.

One of the areas in which research has made great strides in recent years is in studies of the influence of the social environment on the course of schizophrenia. Before reviewing this work, it is necessary to consider briefly the position regarding the inheritance of schizophrenia. If the appearance of schizophrenia was totally determined by specific genes, there would be little point in studying the causative role of the social environment, but the evidence indicates that inheritance accounts for at most 50% of the appearance of schizophrenia.[1] This leaves ample scope for the social environment to exert an influence in the causation of schizophrenia, as well as playing a part in perpetuating the condition once it has appeared. However, there is a major obstacle in the way of studying the role of social factors in the causation of schizophrenia, namely that it is not possible to pick out people who are going to develop the illness before they do so. Thus nearly all studies of the causation of schizophrenia start with the patient who has already developed the characteristic symptoms. Attempts are then made to look backwards over the patient's life and reconstruct features of the social environment believed to be important, such as the early mother-child relationship. Both the lapse of time and the distorting effect of the patient's illness on his own and other's recall of past events make this kind of reconstruction extremely dubious. Several theories concerning the family's role in the causation of schizophrenia have been put forward, but there is very little solid evidence for the truth of any of them.

A more fruitful strategy has been to study the social factors that contribute to an improvement or a worsening of the condition once it has appeared. In the middle of this century a revolution occurred in the treatment of the mentally ill. There was a growing realisation of the harmful effects of retaining patients in mental hospitals for long periods of time, sometimes throughout their lives. This led to a shift in focus of care for the mentally ill from the mental hospital to the community. One consequence of this change in professional attitudes was that the number of hospital beds in the UK occupied by psychiatric patients began to fall. This process was undoubtedly hastened by the introduction of powerful drugs like chlorpromazine which removed the acute symptoms of schizophrenia, but chlorpromazine was introduced into psychiatry in the mid-1950s, after the decline in psychiatric beds had already begun, so that the change in professional attitudes was at least as important as the new drugs in this revolution in care.

Sceptical voices were soon heard questioning the value of the new movement, stimulated by an apparently high rate of readmission, which resulted in the coining of a phrase, the 'revolving door' policy. It appeared that while the new drugs were almost universally successful in treating acute episodes of schizophrenia, their value in preventing further attacks was not so clear-cut. The question of the success of maintenance drug treatment for schizophrenia became an important scientific issue and several careful studies of drugs given by mouth were carried out in the UK and the USA.[2,3] These showed that if patients took their drugs regularly after recovering from an attack of schizophrenia, they considerably improved their chances of remaining free from further attacks. However, about one-third of the patients taking their drugs by mouth as prescribed still suffered further episodes of schizophrenia. The introduction of antipsychotic drugs given by long-acting injections once every two to four weeks raised hopes of an improvement on this figure, since some patients might not absorb sufficient drug from their stomach when taken by mouth. However, comparison of the maintenance effectiveness of drugs given by mouth and by injection showed no advantage for the latter method of administration. The relapse rate in those treated by injections was also about one-third over the course of a year or two.

The causes for the relapse of patients taking regular maintenance drug treatment have now been identified as coming from the patient's social environment. One set of factors that have been studied recently are referred to as *life events*. These are happenings out of the ordinary which are relatively infrequent and which would be expected to have some psychological impact on a healthy person. Life events range from major occurrences, such as births, marriages and deaths, to minor happenings such as acquiring new neighbours. Clearly there are problems in assessing the impact of any event on a particular individual, since what may appear trivial to one peson may be life-shattering to another because of the circumstances in which he is placed. For example, the effect of one's mother-in-law emigrating to another country is entirely dependent on the quality of one's relationship with her. Techniques have now been developed that allow the assessment of the modifying effect of the social context on the impact of an event on a particular individual. These have been applied successfully to the study of depression, but not so far to schizophrenia. However, the simple counting of events, ignoring their specific impact, has thrown light on the causation of attacks of schizophrenia. In this area it is important to distinguish between events that are outside the person's control, termed independent events, and those which could have been brought about by his behaviour, since these might be a product of the illness rather than a cause. For example, changes in a person's behaviour occur even before the appearance of clear-cut schizophrenic symptoms. Behaviours such as lateness at work, irritability and loss of concentration could well lead to dismissal from a job. It would be an error to attribute the occurrence of an attack of schizophrenia a few weeks later to the dismissal. For this reason the most solid evidence rests on the study of independent life events.

It has been discovered that if you ask healthy people about the occurrence of life events in the preceding three months, 14% report experiencing an independent event in each of the four, three-week periods. When patients with a recent attack of schizophrenia are asked the same questions covering a period of three months prior to the appearance of symptoms, a different picture emerges. For three of the three-week periods, the same proportion as among healthy people report the occurrence of an independent event. However, for the three weeks immediately preceding the attack, the proportion with an independent event jumps from 14 to 46%.[4] This finding strongly implicates life events in the causation of attacks of schizophrenia; but before reaching a conclusion it is necessary to view this in the context of other work on the same topic. It has been found that life events are also concentrated in the period before attacks of depression, before heart attacks, and before operations for abdominal pain at which a normal appendix is removed, and that they occur with excessive frequency to mothers just before their children have an accident serious enough to require medical treatment. It appears, therefore, that life events represent a non-specific form of acute stress which may lead to mental illness, physical illness or to accidents. What determines the particular response to a life event must vary from person to person, but in the case of schizophrenia it is likely to be a part of the genetic predisposition which we have discussed above.

A further aspect of life events that has been studied is their relationship to maintenance drug treatment in schizophrenia. It has been found that patients on regular maintenance drugs have an excess of independent life events in the few weeks before an attack of schizophrenia.[5] Thus it appears that acute stress in the form of a life event can break through the protection afforded by maintenance drugs and trigger off an attack of the illness.

Emotional interaction

A form of chronic stress that has now been extensively studied is the emotional atmosphere in the homes of schizophrenic patients. Attention was focussed on this factor by a study carried out at the time of the change in professional attitudes, when many patients were being discharged from psychiatric institutions. Three hundred schizophrenic patients were followed up five years after their discharge from one of three psychiatric hospitals.[6] Among the factors investigated was the kind of home they returned to. It was found that patients who left hospital to live on their own did better in terms of disturbed behaviour and readmission than those who were discharged to parents or to a spouse. This finding suggested that there was something in the emotional interaction between schizophrenic patients and their close relatives that could lead to a worsening of their condition.

In order to investigate this idea, it was first necessary to develop a reliable method of measuring emotional interactions between people. After a number of years a satisfactory instrument was developed, which takes the form of a standardised interview with relatives shortly after the patient is admitted to hospital with an attack of schizophrenia. The relatives chosen for interview are those in closest contact with the patient, in most cases the parents or a spouse. The relative is asked about the patient's recent behaviour and the emotion they express while giving answers is judged both from the content and from aspects of speech such as rate, volume and tone of voice. A measure of what is termed Expressed Emotion (EE) is built up from the number of critical comments made about the patient and the degree of emotional overinvolvement displayed by the relative. This suggests that schizophrenic patients are particularly sensitive to criticism and overinvolvement on the part of their relatives, and that many of them react with a recurrence of their illness.

However, nearly half of those living with critical or overinvolved relatives did not suffer a relapse during the nine month follow-up period. It emerged that they were protected from relapse by two different factors. One was regular maintenance treatment with drugs as already discussed. The other was to do with the amount of time patients and relatives spent in close social contact. This was measured by constructing a time budget of a typical week, on the basis of which patients were divided into those in high contact and in low contact with their relatives. Patients in low contact with high EE relatives have a better chance of remaining well than those in high contact. It is interesting that the amount of time patients spent with low EE relatives did not affect their chance of keeping well.

These findings were repeated, almost figure for figure, in a later study by a different team of research workers,[7] so that we can have considerable confidence in their reliability. The work was taken a step further in the later study, with respect to the factors protecting patients against the harmful effects of living with high EE relatives. It was found that whereas maintenance drug treatment and reduced social contact each gave a measure of protection, when they were combined there was an additive effect and extra protection was achieved. In fact, patients living in high EE homes for whom both protective factors were present had the same small chance of relapse as those living in low EE homes. This result provides clear indications for the management of schizophrenia, but before discussing these it is worth considering a number of other issues that arise from this work.

The first concerns the effectiveness of maintenance drug treatment, which we saw earlier leaves a lot to be desired. It was found in the recent study that even when patients living in high EE homes took regular maintenance drug treatment, about half of them suffered a relapse of schizophrenia in the nine months following discharge from hospital. This shows that a form of chronic stress, a critical or overinvolved atmosphere in the home, is capable of breaking through the protection afforded by drugs. We found above that the same was true of life events, a form of acute stress.

Since schizophrenia was first formulated as a specific disease eighty years ago, it has generally been looked on as an 'endogenous psychosis', that is, a condition which is due to some intrinsic biological malfunction. An alternative view, that it is an extreme psychological reaction to emotional stress, has been put forward vigorously by psychoanalysts. These two contrasting theories have been presented by their champions as mutually exclusive. However, the work discussed above strongly suggests that schizophrenia is a product of the interaction between an inherited biological malfunction and environmental stresses, two of which have now been clearly identified. It is of interest to inquire into the relationship between these two different forms of stress. Recent work on patients not taking regular maintenance drugs has shown that in those living in low EE homes, an excess of life events precedes an attack of schizophrenia, whereas those in high EE homes have the same rate of life events as a member of the general population. Thus an attack of schizophrenia can result from *either* the acute stress of an independent life event *or* the chronic stress of living in a high EE home.[8] Their relationship in patients on regular maintenance treatment has yet to be clarified.

We will now consider the practical issues that are raised by the body of work on social factors that influence the outcome of schizophrenia. It is evident that the prescription of maintenance drug treatment is of considerable value in preventing further attacks of schizophrenia, but is not a sufficient treatment by itself to ensure continuing health. Something also needs to be done about the elements in the patient's social environment which are known to increase the likelihood of a relapse. Unfortunately, there is little that can be done to reduce the occurrence of independent life events since their very nature renders them virtually unavoidable. However, patients can be warned that they need to consult their doctor when a life event is anticipated or has occurred, and it is possible that the impact of the event may be modified by exploration of the emotions it provokes.

Fortunately, there is much more scope for intervention where the emotional environment is concerned. A number of possibilities suggest themselves, including attempting to separate the patient from a high EE relative by various manoeuvres, identifying the patient's behaviour that provokes criticism or overinvolvement and attempting to alter it, and working with the relatives in order to modify their expressed emotion. A trial of these strategies is currently being conducted and preliminary results indicate that it is, indeed, possible for relatives to reduce their critical or overinvolved attitudes, and thereby to move from a high EE to a low EE rating. The outcome for the schizophrenic patient is considerably improved as a result, this being the main justification for years of painstaking research into links between the social environment and the course of schizophrenia.

References

1. Shields J. (1967). The genetics of schizophrenia in historical context. In *Recent Developments in Schizophrenia* (Coppen A. J., Walk A. J., eds.). Ashford: Headley Bros.

2. Leff J. P., Wing J. K. (1971). Trial of maintenance therapy in schizophrenia. *Brit. Med. J.*; **III**: 599–604.
3. Hogarty G. E., Goldberg S. C. (1973). Drug and sociotherapy in the aftercare of schizophrenic patients. *Arch. Gen. Psychiat*; **28**: 54–64.
4. Brown G. W., Birley J. L. T. (1968). Crises and life changes and the onset of schizophrenia. *J. Health Soc. Behav*; **9**: 203–14.
5. Leff J. P., Hirsh S. R., Gaind R., Rohde P. D., Stevens B. C. (1973). Life events and maintenance therapy in schizophrenic relapse. *Brit. J. Psychiat*; **123**: 659–660.
6. Brown G. W., Bone M., Dalison B., Wing J. K. (1966). *Schizophrenia and Social Care.* Maudsley Monograph, No. 17. London: Oxford University Press.
7. Vaughn C. E., Leff J. P. (1976). The influence of family and social factors on the course of psychiatric illness: a comparison of schizophrenic and depressed neurotic patients. *Brit. J. Psychiat*; **129**: 125–37.
8. Leff J. P., Vaughn C. E. (1980). The interaction of life events and relatives' expressed emotion in schizophrenia and depressive neurosis. *Brit. J. Psychiat*; **136**: 146–53.

9
Causes and Treatment of Schizophrenia

Undoubtedly the outlook for schizophrenia and the prospects for research on the disease were transformed by the discovery of effective drug treatments in the early 1950s. Chlorpromazine (Largactil) was introduced by Laborit and Charpentier in 1951. Like many effective treatments in psychiatry it was a serendipitous discovery. These workers were looking for an antiparasitic drug. Chlorpromazine was found to reduce the body temperature and it was, therefore, originally introduced as a means of reducing the temperature for surgical operations. Subsequently, it was found to have some tranquillising effects, and it was used to calm agitated psychiatric patients. Delay and Deniker then discovered that it was active in the treatment of schizophrenia. A number of carefully designed and well controlled clinical trials have demonstrated that chlorpromazine and a number of subsequently introduced 'neuroleptics' with similar pharmacological properties are not only effective in the treatment of acute psychotic episodes, but can also prevent relapse. Thus many patients now receive long-term neuroleptic medication, and there is much evidence that this not only enables patients who otherwise would remain hospitalised to return to the community, but it also reduces the likelihood that they will experience further psychotic episodes for which they will require hospital admission.

The mechanism of action of neuroleptic drugs has been a

lively area of research in the last twenty, and particularly in the last ten years. It was early recognised that this class of compounds can induce some unusual and unexpected side-effects. In particular they cause changes in the control of movement; specifically they reduce spontaneous movements and induce a tendency to rigidity, associated with tremor, which closely resembles the symptoms of Parkinson's Disease (paralysis agitans). The possibility of analysing the mechanism of these changes was opened up by the work of Hornykiewicz in 1961 when he discovered that the brains of patients who had suffered from Parkinson's Disease were depleted of the substance dopamine, by that time recognised as a probable neurotransmitter in certain areas of the basal ganglia of the brain (e.g. caudate nucleus and putamen). The decrease in dopamine concentrations in Parkinson's Disease almost certainly is a consequence of the degeneration of dopamine-containing neurones, i.e. neurones which release dopamine as a neurotransmitter. The location of these neurones within the brain has been precisely defined by applying histochemical techniques, and in Parkinson's Disease it appears that both the nerve cell bodies and their terminals, which contain high concentrations of dopamine, have disappeared. It seems certain that some at least of the features of Parkinson's Disease are due to the failure of dopaminergic transmission resulting from the loss of dopamine-containing cells.

However, the Parkinsonian symptoms induced by neuroleptic drugs are not due to degeneration of dopamine-containing cells. For one thing it is clear that these changes are reversible when drug administration stops. The work of Carlsson established that these drugs impair dopaminergic transmission, not by depleting the stores of dopamine but by interfering with the action of dopamine at the receptor site on the next neurone on which dopamine exerts its effects. All effective 'neuroleptic' drugs, i.e. drugs which have therapeutic effects in schizophrenia, appear to be antagonists of dopamine receptors. Major advances in the past ten years have been the establishment of methods for assessing drug action on dopamine receptors. Several studies have shown that there is a strong correlation between the abilities of various drugs to interact with the dopamine receptor and their efficacy in the treatment of schizophrenia. No other pharmacological action seems to be so closely associated with the clinical improvement. The evidence strongly supports the view that this is the mechanism of the antipsychotic effect of neuroleptic drugs in the treatment of schizophrenia.

The neurochemistry of schizophrenia

Since no unequivocal pathological changes in the brain have yet been identified in schizophrenia, and particularly because some symptoms respond to drug treatment, it is a plausible hypothesis that the basic disturbance is a change in chemical balance, for example a change in one or more of the neurotransmitters in the brain. A number of specific theories have been proposed and all these theories have had their proponents. However, by far the most fertile hypothesis in recent years has been the *dopamine theory*: the view that there is a disturbance of dopaminergic transmission (for example, overactivity of dopamine neurones) in schizophrenia. The attraction of this theory is that it will not only account for the efficacy of certain drugs in the treatment of schizophrenia, but also for the fact that the symptoms of acute paranoid schizophrenia are very closely mimicked in the amphetamine psychosis, a psychosis which occurs in some amphetamine ('speed') addicts, and which has also been provoked in a few volunteer experimental subjects by the administration of large doses of amphetamine. The chemical structure of amphetamine closely resembles that of dopamine, and there is ample evidence that many of the central actions of amphetamine are due to its ability to enhance dopamine release from dopamine-containing neurones; in other words, to induce a functional overactivity of dopaminergic transmission. Thus symptoms of schizophrenia can be provoked by inducing an overactivity of dopamine transmission, and the symptoms of the illness itself can be relieved by the inhibition of dopaminergic transmission by neuroleptic drugs.

According to the dopamine hypothesis, one might expect to find evidence of increased dopamine neurone activity in schizophrenia. There have now been a number of tests of this prediction, but the results of these investigations are consistent in showing that there is no evidence of increased dopamine turnover. This indicates that dopamine neurones are not over-active. Another possibility is that the fundamental change is not in the dopamine neurone itself, but in the dopamine receptors. Techniques for studying dopamine receptors are now well established and there is evidence that in some schizophrenic patients at least there are increased numbers of dopamine receptors. This increase in numbers of dopamine receptors in some patients is the only biochemical difference so far detected between the brains of schizophrenic patients and those of control subjects dying of similar physical illnesses, but without having suffered from schizophrenia.

Structural changes in the brain

While changes in transmission may account for some parts of the schizophrenic syndrome, this does not seem to be the whole story. Although Bleuler considered that in schizophrenia there is no true impairment of the intellect, even in the chronic conditions, evidence has accummulated that in some patients intellectual deterioration does occur. For example, in a proportion of long-term hospitalised patients quite severe defects of temporal orientation are seen.[1] Such patients often do not know how old they are, how long they have been in hospital, or the current year. Such psychological changes have been thought to be characteristic of the organic psychoses, i.e. the dementias, and in this case they are often associated with structural changes in the brain, e.g. cerebral atrophy. It has been widely assumed that such changes do not occur in schizophrenia. However, there is now good radiological evidence to the contrary. One or two studies with the old fashioned technique of air encephalography (which involves the injection of a small amount of air through a lumbar puncture needle in order to provide a contrast outline for the brain and cerebral ventricles) suggested that there are some patients with schizophrenia with severe deterioration who have cerebral atrophy. This was shown by an increase of the size of the cerebral ventricles (fluid filled cavities in the middle of the brain) which reflects loss of brain tissue. Since this technique, being somewhat unpleasant, has not been widely applied to psychiatric patients, these findings have gone largely unnoticed. However, the recent introduction of computerised tomography (CAT scanning) has allowed this question to be re-examined. A number of studies have now demonstrated that some chronic schizophrenic patients apparently have increased ventricular size by comparison with age-matched controls.[2] Whether or not this is a result of the illness or perhaps reflects some predisposing, possibly genetic, factor remains to be determined. When present, these ventricular changes appear to be associated with evidence of intellectual impairment, and with the negative symptoms of schizophrenia (poverty of speech, loss of emotional response and loss of drive). The findings are now being carefully evaluated in postmortem studies.

The earlier investigations of the electrical activity of the brain showed that many schizophrenics have abnormal EEGs, but they have a wide range of individual variation, and no abnormality characteristic of schizophrenia was found. More recently, the introduction of small laboratory computers has made it possible to carry out the analysis of EEGs so that reliable quantitative information can be obtained about characteristics such as the power and extent of different frequency bands in individual patients. In this way Itil was able to show that the computerised records (CEEGs) of schizophrenics differ significantly from those of matched normal control subjects in having on the average more fast (beta) and more slow (delta) activity,[3] so that they were able to identify a specific type of 'schizophrenic CEEG profile'. These observations were confirmed by Fenton and his colleagues who showed further that the CEEGs of schizophrenics depend to some extent on the stage of the illness.[4] In early acute cases the main finding is an abnormality in the temporal lobes of the brain, whereas in deteriorated long-stage hospital cases a general increase in slow activity, which is characteristic of brain atrophy, is the most striking characteristic. Of particular interest are the observations of Itil and his colleagues on the CEEGs of a group of 69 'high-risk' children of schizophrenic parents. Several of these children gave CEEGs of the 'schizophrenic profile' type and in this respect the group of 'high-risk' children differed significantly from a control group of 71 carefully matched children of normal parents. In due course, it should be possible to see if the children with abnormal CEEGs correspond to the 10–14% of the 'high-risk' children who will ultimately develop a schizophrenic psychosis. It is clearly important that this subgroup should be identified, and the early prediction in this way of schizophrenia, based on the computer analysis of EEGs, has far-reaching implications, not only for increasing our understanding of the pathology of schizophrenia, but also for developing effective measures of preventative treatment.

Two syndromes in schizophrenia?

As Crow has pointed out, the above findings raise the possibility that there may be two separate syndromes of pathology in schizophrenia—one associated with a disturbance of neurotransmission, and one with a progressive degenerative process in the brain. It seems possible that these two processes are associated with different types of schizophrenic symptoms. For example, the symptoms that are specifically improved by neuroleptic drugs include those which are often described as positive symptoms (i.e. features whose *presence* is pathological) namely delusions, hallucinations and thought disorder. Negative symptoms, on the other hand, show little response to neuroleptic treatment and often are associated with poor long-term outcome. Thus it seems there may be two components for the pathology of schizophrenia, the first a neurotransmission disturbance (possibly an increase in numbers of dopamine receptors) which is reversible and responds to medication, and the second a more insidious and progressive change which is associated with some structural alteration in the brain (presumably cell loss from some, as yet, unidentified brain area) which is associated with negative symptoms and intellectual impairment, and corresponds to the irreversible component identified by Kraepelin. While the two components may occur separately, they are often present in the same patient, either sequentially or, not uncommonly, simultaneously. In psychoses characterised by positive symptoms only (labelled, the type I syndrome) complete recovery may occur. Such illnesses are often described as psychogenic or reactive psychoses, or 'good prognosis' schizophrenia. The type II syndrome (characterised by negative symptoms) sometimes occurs alone, and in this case is described as 'simple' schizophrenia (a subgroup introduced by Bleuler). In classical or Kraepelinian schizophrenia, episodes of the type I syndrome are followed by the gradual development of the features of the type II syndrome. Thus the delineation of two groups of schizophrenic symptoms, and their possible association with different types of pathology, may be relevant to the issues of diagnosis and outcome posed by Kraepelin and Bleuler's original concepts.

Causation of schizophrenia

It is generally accepted that genetic factors play a part in the causation of schizophrenia. Thus in twin studies a concordant rate (the likelihood that if one twin is schizophrenic the other will also be) is approximately 50% in monozygotic (identical) twins as opposed to 15% for dizygotic (non-identical) twins. This indicates that there is a substantial genetic component; and this is supported by the results of a number of adoption studies which demonstrate that the risk to children of developing schizophrenia is related to the incidence of the disease, not in their adoptive parents, but in their original biological parents. However, it must be noted that the concordance in identical twins falls far short of 100%. This indicates that the disease cannot be a simple inherited disorder of metabolism, and that non-genetic environmental factors must also be considered. The fact that the illness is not present from birth, and commonly develops in the third and fourth decades of life, also requires an explanation in non-genetic terms. One possibility is that the genetic component is a gene which confers susceptibility to a virus infection, since it is known that the susceptibility to virus infections is genetically determined. Schizophrenic symptoms have in the past been noted as occasional sequelae, both of the strange influenza epidemic that swept the world in 1918, and of encephalitis lethargica (Von Economo's disease) which occurred in the early 1920s and which is widely believed to have been due to an unidentified virus.

Some other findings might be consistent with a viral aetiology for schizophrenia. For example it is now well established from a number of studies that people who subsequently become schizophrenic are more likely than the rest of the population to have been born in the early months of the year. A possible explanation of this curious finding is that such patients were exposed when born at this time of year to a virus which can become latent and subsequently reappear. Although other explanations are possible, it is also of interest that there is some evidence for seasonality of onset for the illness, a slight excess of psychotic illness developing for the first time in the early summer. There is, however, little evidence that schizophrenic illnesses are transmitted from one person to another, and a viral hypothesis, although plausible, is as yet speculative. Attempts by Crow and his associates to detect a virus in patients with the disease have demonstrated that samples of cerebrospinal fluid from some patients will induce effects in a cell culture which resemble those caused by some viruses. However, that these effects are caused by a virus rather than by some toxic factor has not been demonstrated, and similar effects are produced by samples from some patients with other psychiatric and neurological diseases.

A detrimental gene responsible for a serious illness such

as schizophrenia would be gradually eliminated from the population by the normal processes of natural selection unless it was associated with some favourable characteristic which tended to increase the frequency of the gene. Since schizophrenia affects about 1% of the population, which is a high rate for a genetically determined disorder, this has raised the question of what the associated favourable characteristic may be. A number of earlier investigators reported a high incidence of mental illness in men of genius and in their families, and more recent genetic studies have given evidence that certain intellectual characteristics are apparently associated with the gene for schizophrenia. Thus in an investigation of the records of a group of 97 adopted children, Heston found a considerably higher level of artistic and other types of talent in 47 children with a schizophrenic parent than in 50 children of normal parents who served as controls. More recently Karlsson[5] found the incidence of schizophrenia to be considerably higher in the nearer relatives of a large group of distinguished writers, poets and scholars than in the general population. He concluded that the favourable characteristic associated with the schizophrenic gene is a form of cerebral arousal that results in intellectual brightness and creative ability, but it can also lead to psychological imbalance as an unfortunate byproduct.

Although there has been some increase in research on schizophrenia in the past ten years, many problems remain unsolved. Questions raised by recent radiological studies of the structural changes in the brain in some schizophrenic patients, and the location of such changes, remain to be answered by postmortem neuropathological studies. The relationship of whatever neuropathological changes are detected to disturbances of dopaminergic transmission has yet to be worked out. Of considerable importance is the question of causation, whether by viral infection or other pathological processes, e.g. autoimmunity. So far relatively little work has been done on the relationship between the psychological changes and the neurohumoural and structural changes which are held to underlie the disease, but recent investigations by Janice Stevens at Washington have confirmed older reports of the occurrence of patchy gliosis (scarring) in the brains of many schizophrenics.[6] The gliosis, which indicates a healed inflammatory process, most often affected midbrain structures which mediate the functions known to be disturbed in schizophrenics, and in some cases the pathological findings could be related to the clinical manifestations found in individual patients. It would appear that further research on similar lines could well lead to the identification of a slow virus or other infective agent and hence to effective methods of treatment and prevention of some of the more prevalent forms of schizophrenia.

References

1. Liddle P. F., Crow T. J. (1984). Age disorientation in chronic schizophrenia is associated with global intellectual impairment. *Brit. J. Psychiat*; **144**: 193–9.
2. Anand K. P., Dewan M. J., Lee S. H., *et al.* (1984). The ventricular system in chronic schizophrenic patients. *Brit. J. Psychiat*; **144**: 172–6.
3. Itil T. M. (1976). In *Schizophrenia Today*, (Kemali D., Bartholini G., Richter D., eds.) pp. 202–9. Oxford: Pergamon Press.
4. Fenton G. (1980). In *Priorities in Psychiatric Research*, (Lader M., ed.) pp. 163–5. Chichester: John Wiley.
5. Karlsson J. L. (1981). Genetic basis of intellectual variation in Iceland. *Hereditas*; **195**: 283–8.
6. Stevens J. (1982). Neuropathology of schizophrenia. *Arch. Gen. Psychiat*; **39**: 1131–9.

10
Research in Child Psychiatry

What are the commonest types of mental disorder occurring in children? Many of the children who are seen by psychiatrists in the Child Guidance clinics are brought by their parents because of behavioural disorders such as tantrums, vandalism, general 'naughtiness' or different forms of overactivity. The parents are often concerned about an overactive child, but the child's overactivity is more likely to be due to underlying anxiety than a direct expression of pathological hyperactivity. Many of the children referred to the Clinics by the schools because of learning failure or possible dyslexia are also restless and overactive in their behaviour, and that is specially marked in children from broken homes or where there are family disturbances causing stress. Their behaviour then may represent a cry for help rather than an inherent mental disorder. In the children referred by their GPs disorders such as not sleeping, bed-wetting or soiling their clothes are common reasons for referral, but behavioural disorders can vary widely in the underlying causal factors. Thus of the children who are caught stealing by shop-lifting the underlying motive may be simply greed, but some children take things they do not really want and their behaviour may then be a reaction to the challenge of doing what is forbidden. In some sections of the community there are even parents who encourage their children to bring home valuables picked up in that way, and the underlying motive of trying to please their parents is then different again. Sexual behaviour such as masturbation used to be a frequent reason for referral by parents, but it is now commonly accepted that that is not a behavioural disorder requiring treatment. Fortunately, the more serious forms of mental disorder in childhood, such as mental subnormality, autism (withdrawal from external reality) and childhood psychoses are relatively rare.

Despite the recognition in recent years that between 5–15% of children in Britain in one year suffer some degree of mental disorder, there are signs that we are moving towards a time when factors that interfere with the mental health of children will be understood well enough for some of their mental disorders to be prevented, and for the course of some of those mental illnesses in adults shown to have their roots in childhood to be modified.

The basis for this belief lies in the part played by research in two spheres. One concerns the accumulation of the vast amount of information about all aspects of childhood built up over the last fifty years. The other is the way research has shaped the subject matter, or child psychiatry. For instance, the subject as a whole has been given structure and form, following careful, scientifically based, classification in an exceedingly complex field. Furthermore, a movement has developed amongst clinicians towards looking, in a systematic way, at how the outcome of treatment can be assessed, and at how the most effective intervention for each individual child can be planned and implemented. The present rate of progress suggests that further work, in the tradition already established, will lead to a reduction in the incidence of some forms of mental disorder in childhood and to more effective intervention in others.

The tradition which has developed over the last twenty years has moved many members of the discipline of child psychiatry to a stage when they handle their subject matter as though it were a young science, whilst maintaining at the same time a sensitive approach to the investigation and treatment of children with mental disorder. Continuing research along lines of work that are already proving fruitful, in the confidence that a scientific approach will be maintained, has opened up the possibility that advances will be made in the next fifty years commensurate with those achieved during the first half of this century in medicine and surgery.

The likelihood that a scientific tradition will remain active in child psychiatry in Britain is supported by the observation that over the last ten years there has developed a steady insistence upon work at a level that merits the description 'scientific'. Such insistence has come, in Britain, from three directions. There has been the inception of the Royal College of Psychiatrists with an active section that shows a keen interest in research and has responsibilities in regard to the training of child psychiatrists. There has also been the establishment in the medical schools of four academic departments of Child Psychiatry. Thirdly, and at a different level, scientific research in child psychiatry has been aided by many advances made recently in the behavioural sciences, particularly ethology and psychology, and by the establishment of working links with workers in these fields.

It is often felt that it is dehumanising to regard child psychiatry as a scientific subject when its essential aim is the relief of disability and suffering, but that need not be so. A scientific approach to the wide range of suffering seen in child psychiatric practice is not incompatible with the exercise of respect, patience and understanding towards those who suffer. Human nature suggests that there will always be a wide range of working methods within the discipline. For instance, at one end of a continuum, there are intuitive clinicians who have a 'feel' about their patients and who are more interested in working with children and their parents, to the benefit of both, than in focussing on the complementary and separate task of testing out the validity of their understanding about the nature of the clinical problems they are treating.

At the other pole, there are those psychiatrists who are primarily investigators and who wish to give their full attention to the task of clarifying the nature of the fundamental processes at the root of mental illhealth in children. So long as there is communication, and respect, between those who are primarily clinicians and those who are primarily investigators, each can gain insights from the other that will bring benefits to their respective spheres of action.

The examples cited below, a very few among many, have been selected to demonstrate the range of research, either as hypothesis testing or conceptualisation, that has played an essential part in increasing our understanding of, and ability to handle, the very complex problems connected with mental disorder in childhood. These examples, therefore, illustrate work that has been 'pivotal' in that it has provided information and ideas that have led clinicians and investigators to make strategic changes in outlook and practice.

The classification of mental disorders in childhood

We have decided to use an example of classification as the first illustration of effective research, in order to illustrate the complex issues involved in handling the subject of mental illness in childhood, where the simple concept of a number of different mental illnesses has long been considered too limiting to be useful.

In any sphere of medicine, an effective and relevant classification clarifies thinking and helps clinicians to communicate with one another. It also distinguishes factors, in themselves unrelated, that commonly contribute to the picture presented when illness strikes. It must be noted, however, that classifications like other useful endeavours can be abused.

In child psychiatry there are some who are reluctant to use any classification because of their fear of the damaging consequences should the child become identified with the label given to his disorder. Children, for example, labelled 'delinquent' may identify with the label, or react violently against it, in such a way that their behaviour becomes delinquent.

A method of classification recently developed minimises

the harmful tendency to label children rather than the disorder from which they suffer, and takes note of a range of factors, referred to as 'axes', that regularly have to be taken into account when a diagnosis is made. The axes show what a particular child has in common with others in a way that allows some of his individuality to stand out. A child, for instance, may have an incapacitating neurotic disorder which can be seen as one axis along which the diagnosis is made. The disorder will be one that he will share with many other children. He will, however, be at a particular stage of general physical and psychological development which he shares with other children—the second axis; he will also have a level of intellectual ability—the third axis. A fourth would describe the particular social and family environment in which he lives and a fifth axis would take into account any concurrent medical condition, as for example, asthma or epilepsy. This multiaxial classification was originally conceived along three axes, but experience has shown it to be reliable[1] and worth developing to the five axes illustrated above.

The multiaxial classification has now been in common use for about ten years. It has not provided unequivocal answers for every diagnostic conundrum and it may well be adapted as experience in its use accumulates. Nevertheless, the conceptual research that led to the idea of a multiaxial classification is of great importance because it has made problems of diagnosis more manageable. The psychiatrist is able to describe a disorder in terms of the behaviour seen at the time of diagnosis and include factors that relate to the constitution of the child, to his level of development and to his environment, without trying to relate them to the way the child is behaving. As a result the label is not biased by any theoretical ideas about peculiarities of constitution, environment or experience that might cause or maintain the disorder. The fact that this classification is found useful by clinicians and researchers of different schools of thought has a valuable political spin off for the subject as a whole. When based on a common description and classification, discussions about clinical issues are likely to be more constructive than discussion confused from the outset by the intrusion of disagreements about the criteria used to arrive at a diagnostic label.

In this tradition the word 'psychiatric disorder' is preferred to mental illness when talking about children; psychiatric disorder being defined as a persistent disturbance of behaviour sufficient to handicap a child in everyday life. The diagnosis of mental retardation, research on which is discussed in another chapter, is seen as a separate condition. The two may occur together, but many mentally retarded children have no psychiatric disorder.

The prevalence of psychiatric disorder in children

It has been common knowledge for some time that disturbed children very rarely seek professional help on their own initiative and that adults seek help on their behalf. Nevertheless, there has been a strong suspicion based on clinical experience that not all adults in charge of disturbed children seek professional help. Therefore, figures about the prevalence of psychiatric disorder in children, worked out from attendance figures at Child Guidance clinics and other agencies, are too low. It needed, however, well thought out research to show unequivocally the full extent to which upsets in behaviour in children, severe enough to be classified as psychiatric disorders, are overlooked, misperceived as naughtiness or laziness, or otherwise explained away.

The results of research over the last ten to fifteen years have shown that, whereas most children have transient upsets in behaviour of a kind that, should they be persistent, would qualify for the label of psychiatric disorder, and whereas the dividing line between transient upsets and psychiatric disorder is blurred, nevertheless, between 5–15% of children are estimated to have psychiatric disorders. Such disorders are severe enough to persist for at least several years and are associated with considerable personal suffering and often with difficulties such as poor scholastic achievement. A much smaller number of children (between 4 and 5 per 10 000) have disorders with symptoms that are different in kind from any shown by ordinary children. The commonest disorder of this group is infantile autism, a condition in which thinking tends to be self-centred and out of touch with objective reality.

The method used to determine prevalence is epidemiology which, in competent hands, is a powerful research tool. Epidemiology is defined as the study of the distribution of disorders within populations and the assessment of how the distribution is affected by the presence of particular environmental circumstances. It may, therefore, be used to show how prevalence may vary over a period of time and to study factors from the environment which may be causal. It is a reliable tool, provided it is used to test defined hypotheses, and provided the particular environmental circumstances selected for the study are defined rigorously so as to be unambiguous, and provided also that the statistical procedures used to assess the data are appropriate. Furthermore, though it requires very clear thinking to use effectively, epidemiology is the only tool which enables us to pick out, from amongst many thousands of possibilities, the circumstances that are most likely to predispose children to different kinds of psychiatric disorder.

A well planned and rigorous study that is a model for the effective use of epidemiology in child psychiatry is that made by Rutter and his associates[2] on ten-year-old children in two populations—one in the Isle of Wight (100 000) the other in a London borough (population 170 000). The hypotheses tested were concerned with finding (a) the prevalence of psychiatric disorder in the two populations and (b) whether various selected environmental circumstances in the family and social scene predisposed children to psychiatric disorder.

The results showed that about 9% of the Isle of Wight children were suffering from a psychiatric disorder, but that the figure was twice as high for the London children. These figures are surprising and disquieting. The information the authors chose to gather about the environment has allowed them to go a long way towards explaining why the figures for London are so high. They showed that in both populations the prevalence of psychiatric disorder was highest for children who came from homes where there was overcrowding and large families, family discord and disruption, and parental illness and criminality. Moreover, the level of disorder in children from non-disadvantaged families in both populations was comparable, but the number of families suffering the disadvantages mentioned above was three times higher in London than in the Isle of Wight. London children, therefore, were more likely to suffer from psychiatric disorder, because many more London families suffered from these disadvantages.

However, as in all research, every finding uncovers fresh questions. In this instance, two questions are foremost. Why are London families more likely to be disadvantaged, and why do some children from disadvantaged families escape, apparently unscathed? Studies to find answers to these questions are currently under way, though far from complete. It should be noted, however, that although the Isle of Wight/London study has shown clearly that certain family circumstances predispose children to psychiatric disorder, it only assesses the prevalence of disorder for these two populations. Prevalence in the whole country or internationally can only be assessed by comparing the results of different studies and making careful extrapolation from all our knowledge to estimate the prevalence in areas not surveyed.

Non-accidental injury in children

Human beings the world over show two contradictory states in regard to caring for children. They are drawn to look after children with love and tenderness, yet there is evidence since history began that children can be mercilessly abused. Despite a description in 1888 of the signs of child abuse, it was not until 1962 that Kempe[3] and his associates published the now classic paper, emotively entitled *The Battered Child Syndrome*, that professional eyes opened. Shock and initial disbelief were followed by a growing acceptance of Kempe's findings, so that now there is an extensive research literature and registers of children at risk.

The physical abuse of children, relabelled in recent years 'Non-Accidental Injury', seemed at first a paediatric problem. However, as the phenomenon has been investigated, it has become apparent that abuse predisposes children to psychiatric disorder and that the management of abusers calls for psychiatric skills. Research—not made easier by the discovery that to work in this area is particularly upsetting—has shown that child abuse is not haphazard, despite evidence that anyone sufficiently stressed by adversity is liable to abuse a child they judge to be uncooperative. People who abuse children share certain characteristics, although a great many people with these features do not abuse children. For example, abusers are most likely to be the parents, step-parents, or others in charge of a child; they are likely to have been abused as children themselves; they frequently function at the emotional level of a young child, and the abuse occurs during outbursts of uncontrolled anger.

Although the research to date is insufficient to allow the prevalence of non-accidental injury to be assessed reliably, conservative estimates suggest that the figure for serious abuse is of the order of 0·1% and that at least 25% of seriously abused children suffer impairment of intelligence as the result of brain damage.

Research so far has shown that we are only beginning to understand how best to help parents who abuse children and the children who have been abused. It has, however, become clear that punishment is singularly ineffective and that programmes aimed at safeguarding the children and educating parents sensitively, but forthrightly, in the art of parenthood have promise.

There are likely to be many reasons why child abuse has not been investigated until today; the shock and disbelief that greeted Kempe's 1962 paper and others in a similar vein shows that human nature, although it would rather conceal such realities, is open to the power of well planned research to shatter illusions. Such power comes, not by trying to prove a point, but rather by acting as devil's advocate and attempting to disprove it. This approach means that the new facts are research findings that are predictable and have repeatedly resisted strenuous efforts to disprove them. So long as the climate of opinion is in favour of scientific research, unpalatable or unexpected facts have a chance of being accepted and built into our idea of reality sooner rather than later.

Pivotal concepts in child psychiatry

The foregoing remarks on research—and on epidemiology as a tool in the hypotheses testing phase of research—has emphasised the need for relevant and clearly formulated hypotheses. Hypotheses, however, arise from some intuition, theoretical idea or concept based on our own or other people's experience. In this section some concepts are discussed that have proved influential over the last forty years, either because they have inspired investigators to think out hypotheses worth testing, or because they were—or are—of practical use in helping clinicians to predict how children might respond to the interventions they—or Fate—prescribe. It must be remarked that these two different uses of concepts and theory provide ammunition for many a battle between psychiatrists, who are primarily investigators, and those who are primarily clinicians, because the latter tend to continue to use concepts they have found useful in understanding clinical problems well in advance of supportive evidence. Child psychiatry abounds in concepts and theories which clinicians find useful—and so keep alive—but which investigators view with scepticism. Psychoanalytic theories are outstanding examples. The drawback is that they are expressed in metaphors about feelings, attitudes and hypothesised psychic structures that defy attempts to translate them into items that can be observed and quantified, an essential step before any hypotheses can be tested.

Psychoanalytic theories have been found useful to clinicians because they deal with issues concerning relationships and the passions they arouse. Such theories, however, are no longer the only ones in this area. Over the last forty years scientists the world over have become increasingly interested in the effects of environment on all aspects of man's behaviour and psychological development, from infancy onwards. The movement has been stimulated by the steady growth of ethology (the study of human character) and the interest in the behaviour of man taken by ethologists in recent years. All this work has produced a substantial body of research on the effects of many aspects of the environment, including topics such as the effects of rapidly changing environments, effects of losses of different kinds (which has led to the recognition of the syndrome of mourning) and the effects of crowding and isolation. Child psychiatrists have made significant contributions to this movement, although as a body they have been prudently critical of conclusions that might be premature. Not surprisingly, the concepts and theories about man and his environment that have sparked off the range of hypotheses investigated have been disparate and unintegrated. Despite this, child psychiatry as a subject has kept abreast of concepts and findings that are relevant for children so that, after some twenty years of grappling with apparently contradictory and confusing research findings, child psychiatrists are beginning to discover some guiding rules of thumb based upon reliable and reproduceable research findings rather than on opinion. Findings, for example, that infants and parents are not part of one another, but have to build a partnership and form a bond, which may happen rapidly or take an appreciable time; that children need fathers as well as—and perhaps as much as—mothers; that children mourn losses of significant objects, places and above all people; and that psychological development takes place as a result of continual interaction between constitutional and genetic factors on the one hand and environmental ones on the other, so that an optimal environment will tend to diminish the effects of constitutional weaknesses which deprived environments will exacerbate.

The child psychiatrist who has contributed most to a comprehensive theory of the effects of interpersonal relationships on the psychological development of man is

John Bowlby; both by his careful scientific exposition of attachment theory[4,5,6] and by his outspoken and often controversial views. Whatever the ultimate findings, his work, because it is phrased in ways that invite the derivation of testable hypotheses, has the power to stimulate research in new and important areas.

Research and the changing role of the child psychiatrist

The recognition of the inescapable, though not yet fully understood, part played by the environment in a child's wellbeing has led to the recognition that an essential aspect of the treatment of children with psychiatric disorder, is to see—for at least some of the time in all instances and for as much as is humanly possible in others—that the child's surroundings are experienced by him as secure, interesting and consistent. Such a recognition has gone hand-in-hand with changes in the way child psychiatrists see their role. They have moved from the traditional Child Guidance model towards working more closely and actively with those in charge of the child's environment (e.g. parents, teachers, and the staff of residential homes for children) in order to help in the creation of a more therapeutic environment for the children whose behaviour is causing concern. In making this shift child psychiatrists have played a part together with members of other disciplines working with children in the development of several new skills. Two of these are consultation and family therapy. In consultation the trained consultant works with a consultee (e.g. a teacher or group of teachers) who is concerned about one or more of the children in his—or her—care. The consultant helps the consultee identify specific sources of stress for the child within their working environment (in this instance the school); and discusses ways in which such stress can be reduced, without undue strain on the resources of the school. In family therapy—at its best—the therapist enables the members of a family to discover how to behave towards each other so that life for everybody at home is more comfortable, and the members become more effective in their lives outside. There are many reports of significantly beneficial changes in family relationships and in the wellbeing of disturbed children, as a result of family therapy. Notwithstanding, more hypothesis-testing research and studies of long term outcome are needed in this difficult field before it is known which kind of families will benefit most from which kind of family intervention and, indeed, the instances where family therapy should not be practised.

The remarks about family therapy also apply to consultation. Both these examples show the way child psychiatrists as a body are prepared to adapt their practice as a result of information which comes from exploring new fields and subjecting the early discoveries in any area to stringent examination before assessing their ultimate worth.

Research and prevention

The argument put forward in this chapter is that child psychiatrists, through undertaking research and applying other people's research findings in a scientific way, have brought order and increased knowledge to their subject. In this way they have reached the stage when prevention of some forms of psychiatric disorder in children will be possible in the foreseeable future.

As mentioned above, all psychiatric disorders have an environmental component. Currently it appears that it will be possible to define the elements required to set up a healthy environment for different kinds of children; but to produce such an environment in areas where there are high rates of psychiatric disorder will entail changes of attitude and custom on the part of legislators and teachers, parents and guardians, and the public at large.

It is difficult to predict in what way child psychiatrists should engage in the task of public education. Whatever their role in the future, they are likely to continue along two lines of action. In the first place there is a great deal more research waiting to be done in areas that have already been opened up, which will clarify issues such as the effects of family discord in children of different temperaments. Secondly, they can make clear expositions to a wide public of substantiated research findings so that governments, educators, and others concerned about children become aware of new facts about psychological development that have the power to resist determined attempts to disprove them.

References

1. Rutter M., Shaffer D., Shepherd M. (1975). *A Multiaxial Classification of Child Psychiatric Disorders.* Geneva: World Health Organization.
2. Rutter M., Cox A., Tupling C., Berger M., Yule W. (1975). The prevalence of psychiatric disorder. *Brit. J. Psychiat*; **126**: 493–507.
3. Kempe C. H., Silverman F. N., Stede B. F., Droegmuller W., Silver H. K. (1962). The battered child syndrome. *J. Amer. Med. Assoc*; **181**: 17.
4. Bowlby J. (1969). Attachment. In *Attachment and Loss.* Vol. I. London: The Hogarth Press.
5. Bowlby J. (1973). Separation, anxiety and anger. In *Attachment and Loss*, Vol. II. London: The Hogarth Press.
6. Bowlby J. (1980). Loss, sadness and depression. In *Attachment and Loss*, Vol. III. London: The Hogarth Press.

11
Research in Mental Handicap

Children show a wide range of variation in the way they develop. Some are ready to walk and talk at a relatively early age, others develop much more slowly, or their development of different types of mental function is uneven, so that they fall behind at school, their social life is restricted and in a competitive world they tend to get left behind. In some cases, the mental retardation is so severe that they are never able to engage in useful employment or to be accepted as normal members of society. Mental handicap (synonyms: mental retardation, mental deficiency, mental subnormality) implies a permanent impairment of the intellect sufficiently severe to prejudice normal existence in the community. Mental handicap is thus a social as well as a medical and psychological concept: it reflects both the lack of intelligence of an affected individual and the complexity of the society in which he lives.

The investigation of mental handicap has been greatly helped by the development of standard tests for assessing intelligence, which can be done by recording the responses to standardised verbal and non-verbal tasks. The results are expressed as intelligence quotients (IQs) which, in essence, compare the performance of an individual to that of the population to which he belongs. Intelligence scales such as the Stanford-Binet or the Wechsler are so constructed that the distribution of IQs is roughly normal and so resembles that of continuously variable characteristics such as height. Half the population have IQs in the average range of 90 to 109, while a quarter have an IQ of less than 90. Those with a lower IQ of 50 to 70, who make up 1·8% of the population, are classed as 'mildly retarded' and many of them do not need medical care or any special educational provision. Those with an IQ below 50, about 0·4% of the population, are severely subnormal. They always need special education and often they require medical care in a hospital or in the community.

In the past, mental handicap was not clearly distinguished from the mental illnesses which arise later in life and in which there is no impairment of intelligence. The mentally handicapped were, therefore, often put in the mental asylums together with the mentally ill. The severely subnormal were regarded traditionally as suffering from a hereditary condition resulting from a defective 'major gene' or from a pathogenic environmental factor such as meningitis or birth injury, while the mildly retarded were seen as a different 'subcultural group' belonging to the general population. This distinction can no longer be maintained. Thus some patients with a dominantly transmitted genetic disorder may be severely retarded, while other affected members of the same family are virtually free from symptoms, with their intelligence unimpaired. Similarly, environmental factors such as German measles infection before birth (rubella embryopathy) may give rise to mental defect ranging in severity from virtual normality to the grossest handicap. When they die and their brains are examined at postmortem, the more severely retarded generally show more extensive morphological abnormalities of the brain,[1] but there is no evidence of a distinction between pathological and subcultural types of mental subnormality.

Mental retardation can result from the operation of adverse genetic or adverse environmental factors. Genes and environmental factors will both impair intelligence if they act at a molecular level to produce structural or metabolic abnormalities which interfere with the normal functions of the brain. Furthermore, genetic and environmental factors can act together via the same common pathological pathway: for example, both can cause the bilirubin level in the blood to rise to a toxic level which causes irreversible brain damage in young infants. In a high proportion of cases the mental handicap cannot be attributed to a single cause, either genetic or environmental. In a substantial proportion, probably a majority of cases, the mental retardation is the result of the interaction of a multiplicity of genetic and environmental factors which, if acting alone, might well have been successfully overcome by the brain with its capacity to resist even severe insults. What matters in practice is to identify the pathogenic factors and to counteract their harmful effects.[2]

Table 1

CAUSES OF MENTAL RETARDATION

	%
Perinatal disorders	18·5
Chromosome abnormalities	17·5
Malformations	7·5
Infections of the CNS	6·6
Metabolic disorders	3·1
Other genetic disorders	2·4
Injury, poisoning	1·5
Indeterminate causes	42·9
Total	100

Right up to the beginning of World War II published work on the causes of mental retardation amounted to little more than guesswork often based on prejudice and preconceived ideas. The systematic scientific investigation of the causes may be said to have been pioneered by the late Lionel Penrose who made a clinical and genetic study of 1280 cases in 1938. A similar study of 1416 cases made on similar lines in England, Germany and Switzerland is given in summary in Table 1. The cases attributed to 'metabolic disorders' include, for example, conditions such as untreated congenital cretinism, untreated phenylketonuria and storage diseases affecting the brain. 'Other genetic disorders' include many syndromes, often associated with morphological changes, in which no metabolic defect has as yet been identified. Both antenatal and postnatal infections of the central nervous system (CNS) can result in mental deficiency. Malformations are determined either genetically or by environmental factors such as toxic substances (teratogens) in the mother's diet: congenital malformations arise during the first three months of pregnancy. In a high proportion of the cases examined the cause of the mental retardation was found to be 'indeterminate'.

More recent research has confirmed the importance of maintaining a healthy environment for the growing embryo during pregnancy. Injury to the fetus arising from German measles infection during pregnancy can be prevented by vaccination, and it is now well recognised that the pregnant mother should not take any drugs such as the sedative thalidomide which can cause serious fetal damage. Care should also be taken to avoid possible injury to the fetus through the toxic effects of excessive smoking or alcohol abuse. A few years ago a number of drugs were widely used as pregnancy tests (Amenorone, Primodos, etc.), but research carried out by Isabel Gal showed that their use was closely associated with congenital cerebral malformations such as hydrocephalus in the infants that were born, and with the help of the Committee on Safety of Medicines the use of these drugs for this purpose has now been banned. Research of this kind has clearly been of value in preventing the occurrence of certain kinds of mental retardation.

One of the main lines of research in this field has been the biochemical investigation of children suffering from mental subnormality, and this has now resulted in the recognition of more than fifty different conditions in which mental subnormality is associated with a genetically determined metabolic disorder. The nature of the biochemical defect may be determined by the identification of an abnormal metabolite in the blood or urine, or by the response to different kinds of dietary or drug treatments.[3] It would not be possible in the space available here to give an adequate account of all the relevant research, much of it highly technical, which has been carried out on the investigation of metabolic disorders of this kind. The nature of this research is, therefore, illustrated by the following accounts of the investigation of two relatively common conditions, cretinism (or hypothyroidism) and phenylketonuria, in which research has finally led to the development of effective forms of treatment.

Cretinism

Cretinism is a disorder in which mental deficiency occurs in association with a general dwarfing of the body. It is characterised by retarded skeletal growth, arrested sexual development, coarse facial features with broad nose and enlargement of the tongue, as well as mental retardation and other neurological defects. Cretinism used to be endemic in many parts of the world, especially in areas such as the valleys of the Alps where goitre was common, and it was once regarded as the main cause of mental backwardness. In French and German the terms 'cretin' and 'idiot' are synonymous. While still a problem in parts of South-East Asia, endemic cretinism has now largely disappeared in the countries that are economically more advanced.

Endemic cretinism is believed to result from a severe deficiency of iodine in the pregnant mother at an early stage of fetal development, but other factors are probably involved. Other types of cretinism associated with inborn metabolic errors affecting the thyroid glands and accompanied by goitre have also been described. However, numerically much the most important today is congenital non-goitrous cretinism with maldevelopment of the thyroid glands, which fail to secrete the amount of thyroxin required for normal growth and development. This disorder has an estimated incidence in Europe of about 1 in 4000 births and it is probably the commonest endocrine disorder in infants. It is generally accepted that the outlook for intelligence in these hypothyroid infants is better if treatment is started soon after birth. In a survey of many centres it was found that if treatment was started from 7 to 12 weeks after birth little more than a third of the patients had an IQ greater than 90 while nearly 40% had an IQ lower than 75. If treatment started before the age of 6 weeks, however, more than half the affected infants had an IQ over 90 and only 11% below 75. Early treatment thus improves the prognosis significantly, but even early treated patients show some neurological abnormalities. Not unexpectedly, in at least some cases, irreversible injury to the brain has occurred before birth, since the fetus depends on its own rather than its mother's thyroid for normal development. Often, some functioning thyroid tissue is still present at birth and hypothyroidism develops over a period which may range from days to years.

The case for early treatment is greatly strengthened by experimental work with animals, which has established that thyroid deficiency before birth or in early postnatal life leads to a retardation of brain growth and defective formation of the myelin sheaths of the nerve cells. Nerve cell formation is affected and the development of the cell branches and of the nerve terminals is retarded. Thyroid hormone has been found to be important, not only for the formation of the normal numbers of synapses, but also for the development of the synaptic organisation and of the neurotransmitter systems.[4]

To safeguard the normal development of the brain, early treatment of hypothyroidism is thus essential but, unfortunately, the diagnosis of hypothyroidism is difficult in the newborn. In the majority of patients the classical signs of the disease, such as the characteristic appearance of the face, large tongue, protuberant abdomen, large fontanelle and dry skin do not become apparent until later, while the presenting symptoms such as lethargy, constipation, feeding difficulties and prolonged jaundice are not specific for hypothyroidism. Population screening of the newborn, by assay of blood thyroxin and thyrotropin, therefore, offers the best chance of early detection and treatment, and this has been or is being introduced in most

European countries.[5] Treatment with oral thyroxin is relatively simple and adequate doses would prevent intellectual deterioration, but even with the best organised screening programmes there would be a delay of 2–3 weeks before a case is diagnosed and treatment can be started. Careful assessment at the time of diagnosis and throughout childhood will then determine if this inevitable delay and the prenatal lack of thyroid hormone have produced changes which cannot be reversed even though further damage is prevented. However, over-treatment must be avoided, as there is now ample evidence from animal work and clinical observations that excess of thyroid hormone is harmful to the developing brain and in young infants may even be life-threatening. At present the extent to which a child with congenital hypothyroidism will benefit from early treatment cannot be predicted precisely, but in the majority of cases the gain in intellectual competence, physical well-being and the general quality of life are likely to be substantial.

Phenylketonuria

It was in 1934 that the young mother of two mentally retarded children brought them to a clinic at the University Medical School in Oslo and asked if they could be examined, since their urines had a peculiar musty smell. The examination was carried out by a chemical pathologist, Dr Fölling, whose first thought that the children might have a urinary infection proved to be wrong. He then tested the urines with one or two reagents and found to his surprise that they gave a deep green colour with ferric chloride. Since he could not recognise the substance giving this reaction, he asked the mother to come back with 20 litres of the children's urine for him to investigate, and finally he succeeded in isolating an abnormal metabolite, phenylpyruvic acid.

This was the start of an investigation which established for the first time a hereditary form of mental retardation, definitely associated with a specific biochemical abnormality. Besides the mental deterioration and their peculiar odour, children with phenylketonuria can be recognised by their tendency to fair hair and pale colouration of the skin. Genetic studies showed that the condition is attributable to a single recessive gene and it was noted that many of them suffer from epileptic seizures and increased muscle tone, but the degree of mental retardation varies greatly from one case to another.

Fölling's investigations showed that phenylketonurics have an excessively high level of the normal amino acid phenylalanine in the blood. Phenylalanine is normally oxidised in the body to form tyrosine, but phenylketonurics lack the enzyme that is needed for this reaction and this is their primary inborn biochemical defect. Since the phenylalanine ingested in the diet is not metabolised in the normal way, it tends to accumulate in the body fluids and tissues where it forms metabolites such as phenylpyruvic acid which are not found in significant amounts in normal subjects.

While the nature of the enzyme deficiency and the consequently distorted metabolic pattern in phenylketonuria is now well understood, it is not so clear how precisely these biochemical aberrations affect the development and function of the brain. Basic research on the normal development of the brain has led to a better understanding of the way in which growth-restricting factors affect the nature and extent of the ultimate deficits, and it appears that these depend not only on the severity and duration of action of the growth-restricting factors, but also on the developmental stage of the brain at which they operate. The period known as the 'growth spurt' from the last 3 months of pregnancy to about 18 months to 2 years after birth, when the nerve cells are developing at a high rate, is a time of maximum sensitivity to factors such as malnutrition, hormonal imbalance and growth-restricting conditions resulting from inborn metabolic defects, as in phenylketonuria. These influences may be mitigated or aggravated by other supervening genetic and environmental factors, so that the ultimate deficit can vary greatly in different subjects with the same primary metabolic error.[6]

In 1951 the first systematic attempts were made to achieve the effective treatment of children with phenylketonuria. It appeared that this might be done by restricting the intake of phenylalanine in the diet so that the level in their blood would not become so high. Special diets were, therefore, devised in which most of the protein was replaced by a synthetic mixture of other amino acids in appropriate proportions, or by a protein hydrolysate from which the phenylalanine had been removed by chemical means. In principle this treatment is beautifully simple, but in practice numerous problems were encountered. Since phenylalanine is an essential amino acid, the diet must contain sufficient phenylalanine for normal growth and development, and it soon became apparent that its complete elimination from the diet could result in severe deficiency disorders. The intake of phenylalanine, therefore, needs to be carefully adjusted to avoid either excess or deficiency by regular monitoring of the blood level of phenylalanine. This is comparatively straightforward, but the effectiveness of the diet used must also be determined by psychological and educational assessment of the patients in comparison with normal children.

While it is agreed that it is essential to treat all phenylketonurics in early childhood, it is not yet clear at what age, if any, it is safe to discontinue treatment. To decide this point it is necessary to measure changes in IQ occurring in children who for one reason or another have abandoned the special diet. In an investigation of this kind there could be artefacts due to spontaneous variation or other causes and it is, therefore, necessary to compare the IQ changes in the patients with the changes in a controlled group of normal children. Such data on normal children are fortunately available, having previously been collected in the course of projects of pure research in child psychology, although their relevance to the treatment of a metabolic disorder could not have been foreseen at the time when they were made. In a number of studies of this kind, the performance of phenylketonuric children has been found to decrease if they are taken off their special diet. It would appear that a raised blood phenylalanine level can still be harmful, at least to some phenylketonurics in later childhood and after the time of the early brain growth spurt. A reasonable conclusion is that they should continue their dietary treatment beyond the age of 8 years, although a measure of dietary relaxation can probably be tolerated. Further research is now needed to try to identify those children who should remain on the special diet and those who can safely be taken off.

Treatment with a low phenylalanine diet is effective but onerous, because so little natural protein can be allowed. The children tend to rebel against the dietary restriction involved and behavioural problems are frequent when they are treated in this way. An alternative method of treatment now being investigated is to give a normal diet together with a plant enzyme which acts in the gut to remove the phenylalanine liberated there from the dietary protein. Preliminary studies have shown that capsules containing the plant enzyme are effective when administered *in vivo*, but further evidence must be obtained on the safety of the preparation before it can be recommended for long-term use in man.

The clinical investigation of phenylketonurics has shown that, while most of them have the illness in the classical form with a very high blood phenylalanine level, there are others who are less severely affected; their blood phenylalanine levels are only moderately raised and in some cases there has been no intellectual deterioration even though they have not been treated. This is because in those patients the enzyme deficiency responsible for the condition is incomplete. Measurements of enzyme activity in phenylketonurics have shown that the condition is genetically heterogeneous and the extent of the inborn enzyme deficiency varies in different subjects. Such measurements of enzyme activity have also proved useful in controlling treatment and reducing the harmful effects of dietary indiscretions. It is now generally agreed that phenylketonurics whose treatment starts within a month of birth and is well controlled can achieve normal intelligence. Sometimes when their home environment is unsatisfactory and there is poor dietary control the results of treatment are disappointing, but intelligent, caring parents who provide a stimulating home environment are also likely to succeed with the diet and achieve a satisfactory outcome.

If an untreated phenylketonuric girl becomes a mother, the fetus is almost always seriously affected by her high phenylalanine level. Intrauterine growth is retarded and such children are born with serious defects. Phenylketonuric women who have been treated from birth and are, therefore, of normal intelligence may want to have children. To minimise risks to the fetus, it is now recommended that the mother's blood phenylalanine level is controlled, starting before conception and continuing right through the pregnancy. So long as the marriage partner is not heterozygous for phenylketonuria, which can also be tested, the children should then be normal.

Those involved in treating phenylketonurics are apt to be reproached for the increased 'genetic burden' created when patients grow up and, having been treated, are well enough to marry and pass on their harmful genes. In actual fact, calculations based on gene frequencies in the general population show clearly that the effect on future generations will be small and that equilibrium will not be reached for many generations. The apparent ethical dilemma is based on a misunderstanding of the epidemiology of rare recessive disorders of this kind.

Conclusions

Some types of research with mentally retarded patients, as for example the development of new methods of behaviour therapy or rehabilitation, may help to alleviate their condition here and now but will not, in general, help to eliminate the cause of the handicap or lead to prevention. Conversely, long-term basic research on the causation and prevention of brain disease may benefit future generations, but it usually does nothing for those handicapped now, including any patients who may be investigated in the course of the research project. Clearly a balance has to be struck: we must neither prejudice the wellbeing of those not yet born by refraining from research on patients who are not likely to benefit personally nor, on the other hand, must we ask mentally handicapped patients to accept unreasonable discomforts or risks for the sake of others when there is no commensurate benefit to themselves.

At present funds for the health services in general and for medical research in particular are limited, and it is often questioned whether any of the limited financial and manpower resources available should be allocated for long-term basic research. Some hold that no research should have any priority while the essential care of many mentally handicapped patients falls below acceptable minimum standards, but this argument is based on misconceptions. Only a small proportion of the budget for the health services is allocated to research and very little of this to mental health research. For a number of disorders, including phenylketonuria, rubella embryopathy, and kernicterus associated with jaundice due to Rhesus haemolytic disease of the newborn, the cost of diagnosis, treatment and prevention is considerably less than the cost of caring for the handicapped children who would grow up in the absence of preventive measures. The cost of the basic research that made prevention of this type possible is less still, and of an altogether smaller order of magnitude than that of treatment or life-long custodial care. However, the argument in favour of research, treatment and prevention must not be based on cost-effectiveness alone. It would be invidious to put a monetary value on the improvement in the quality of life when mental subnormality is prevented. Even if the care of a mentally retarded patient were cheaper than diagnosis and effective treatment, this would surely not undermine the case for active prevention of the mental handicap.

Those called upon to finance medical research are sometimes faced with the apparently conflicting claims of 'pure' research to advance knowledge which may have no immediate application, and 'applied' research where any positive results can have immediate use. But this dilemma is unreal—the problem is not one of priorities but one of balance. Without the backing of pure research, applied research is apt to be wasteful or even unsound, while pure research in medical science cannot for long flourish in isolation without the stimulus of seeing any discoveries applied where feasible for the benefit of patients.

Phenylketonuria and congenital cretinism illustrate how successful treatment can be based on the application of advances made by research. About 150–200 phenylketonuric and hypothyroid infants born every year in the United Kingdom will now grow up essentially free from mental handicap. This is gratifying, but much still remains to be done. For example, according to the Commons Select Committee on Social Services 5000 infant deaths, and a greater number of mental handicaps, could be prevented by improved maternity services. Certainly, poor maternal health increases the risk of maldevelopment of the infant's brain both before and after birth. The limited resources available to the National Health Service are the major obstacle to the implementation of the Committee's recommendations and of other proposals aimed at improving mental health. The most effective use of whatever resources there are is, therefore, essential and this means that adequate provision for research is not a frill or luxury, but should be an integral part of any programme for improved patient care.

Ultimately, decisions about resource allocations rest with the community. If the will exists, the way is open to a substantial reduction in the prevalence of mental handicap before the end of the century.

References

1. Crome L., Stern J. (1972). *Pathology of Mental Retardation*. London: Churchill Livingstone.
2. Reid A. H. (1983). Psychiatry of mental handicap: a review. *J. Roy. Soc. Med*; **76**: 587–92.
3. Cockburn F., Gitzelmann R., ed. (1982). *Inborn Errors of Metabolism in Humans*. Lancaster: MTP Press.
4. Patel A. J., Balázs R., Smith R. M., Kingsbury A. E., Hunt A. (1980). Thyroid hormone and brain development. In *Multidis-*

ciplinary Approach to Brain Development (Dibenedetta C., Balázs R., Gombos G., Porcellati G., eds.) pp. 261–77. Amsterdam: Elsevier North-Holland.
5. Bickel H., Guthrie R., Hammarsen G. (1980). *Neonatal Screening for Inborn Errors of Metabolism.* Berlin: Springer.
6. Bickel H. (1980). Phenylketonuria: past, present, future. *J. Inher. Metab. Dis*; **3**: 123–32.

12
Mental Disorder in Old Age

The problems of old age have loomed increasingly large on the social and medical scenes in the more advanced countries during the past half century and they are now assuming growing importance in the less developed countries. As living standards and the quality of medical care improve, mortality in infancy and in adult life decrease, and there is usually an associated decline in the birth rate. The ageing of the population is, therefore, an unavoidable concomitant of increasing affluence. It has been estimated that if present trends should continue, in twenty years' time those aged 60 years and over will account for about 10% of the world's population.

The mental diseases to which old people are liable constitute one of the most urgent medical problems confronting contemporary society. Whereas physical illnesses such as cardiac or respiratory disease impose some restraints or limitations on the manner in which old people live, it is the progressive forms of mental decline that threaten their autonomy and often cause them to become helplessly dependent upon others. Many surveys have demonstrated that, given some measure of support, physical handicaps, even when serious, will not prevent old people continuing to live at home or within the community. It is when intelligence and personality begin to decline and disintegrate that independence comes under threat. And with the increasing trend for women to find employment outside the home, the number available to provide care and support for aged relatives becomes even more restricted.

The frequency with which some forms of mental decline occur in later life has probably generated some of the pessimism with which senescence has been regarded down the ages. At a conservative estimate, approximately 21% of those in the community aged 65 and over will be found to be suffering from a recognisable mental disorder and the proportion affected rises steeply with increasing age.[1] In fact, in all countries from which factual information is available, the prevalence of mental disorder reaches a peak in late life.

This must have been noted many centuries ago, and it probably explains the gloom, pessimism and foreboding with which old age has been regarded by most societies that have left a written historical record. Eulogies of old age such as that in Cicero's *De Senectute* have been exceptional. Most of the accounts resemble those of Menander in ancient Greece:

> 'The man who stays too long dies disgusted; his old age is painful and tedious; he is poor and in need. Whichever way he turns he sees enemies; people conspire against him. He did not go when he should have gone; he has not died a good death.'

The famous medical scientist of the 18th century Albrecht Von Halle complained of the bitterness of old age, its solitude, despair and its end in death. The assumption behind all those accounts was that every kind of mental disorder in old age causes the individual to decline without hope of relief into a mere ghost of his original self.

Treatable and chronic illnesses

One of the most striking and significant achievements of modern research into the psychiatry of old age has been the demonstration that the commonest forms of mental illness found among the aged in the community (as distinct from those in hospitals and other institutions) are emotional disorders such as depression and states of anxiety. Unlike the states of progressive mental deterioration denoted by the term 'dementia', which often prove irreversible when they first appear at an advanced age, these emotional illnesses can always be mitigated and sometimes cured.[2] Very rarely now do aged people who suffer in this way have to spend long periods of their remaining lives in hospitals, although this was a common fate until a few decades ago.

The same statement can be made of the neuroses which are found in a substantial minority of elderly people, and the paranoid and schizophrenic illnesses. The majority of patients who suffer from this last group of disorders are particularly liable to be mistaken for cases of cerebral degenerative disease because of their strangely isolated life, often compounded by deafness, their bizarre persecutory delusions and hallucinations and their hostile behaviour. Until some thirty years ago those affected were unable to leave hospital and became chronic patients. Nowadays the majority can be treated with the aid of the modern drugs that keep the symptoms of the most serious forms of mental disorder in check, and so they can continue to live in the community.

Of the 21% of individuals aged 65 and over with mental disorders, approximately two-thirds suffer benign illnesses which are amenable to treatment. They are being recognised to an increasing extent for what they are, but there remains a great tide of human distress among the elderly which goes unrecognised. For example, consummated or 'successful' suicides reach a peak in old age and it is men who are mainly affected. Most such old people have emitted distress signals, many have suffered bereavement or a decline in physical health and have been to see their doctors for a variety of complaints. And treatment given in good time would probably have averted suicide in the majority of cases.

Accurate diagnosis of these cases can present difficulties, because severe emotional disorders give rise to benign and reversible impairments in memory, orientation, intellectual functioning and even deterioration of habits that may cause them for limited periods to resemble the forms of mental decay for which there are at the present time no treatments of proven value.

The well preserved elderly and those subject to mental decline

The modern era in the scientific study of dementia began with clinical observations which established that not all forms of mental illness in old age will pursue the same irrevocable course towards rapid decline and death. They showed that there are a number of distinct illnesses, each with fairly characteristic patterns of clinical presentation, course and outcome. The disorders fall broadly into two main groups. The first group contain the depressions, manias, neuroses and paranoid illnesses of old age. The expectation of life of those who suffer from these disorders is identical with or similar to that of individuals of comparable age in the general population. And when kept under observation over many years, the intellectual functions and personalities of these individuals are found to have remained intact. In the second main group comprising the senile dementias and those forms of intellectual and personality decline due to strokes, the life expectation proved to be only 20–25% of the norm. Those patients enter a course of progressive decline, excepting that small minority of cases in which specific and remediable causes of dementia come to light and can be effectively treated.

The first group appeared to be variants of similar disorders prevalent in earlier life, whose mode of expression is modified by the psychological and physical background of old age. The fact that the structural characteristics of the brain in individuals of the first group do not differ from those found in mentally healthy old people in late life confirms this interpretation. In the second group, distinctive pathological changes are invariably found in the brain. Such changes in the brain are not exclusively confined to those with senile dementia and dementia due to strokes. But the constancy and intensity of the cerebral changes in each of these two disorders established that there is a close link between mental changes evident during life and the pathological alterations found in the brain after death.[3]

It has been known for a considerable time that changes of a qualitatively similar kind are to be found in the brains of well preserved people of advanced age. For a period of decades this tended to obscure the true significance of the changes first described by the psychiatrist and neuropathologist Alzheimer in cases with a certain form of premature senility, which came to be known as Alzheimer's disease. When quantitative measurements were applied about fifteen years ago, both to the mental changes manifest during life and the alterations in the brain whose density and distribution could be estimated by relatively simple techniques, the situation was seen in a different light. The investigation of large groups of well preserved, mildly demented and severely demented old individuals, using psychological measures during life and brain pathology after they had died, established that the amount of measurable alteration in brain pathology was proportionate to the severity of mental deterioration that had been recorded. A relationship of this nature has now been demonstrated in both of the two main forms of dementia in old age: senile dementia of Alzheimer's type (so named because the pathology was identical in respect of cerebral changes to that described by Alzheimer in cases of precocious senility) and that due to multiple strokes.

The 'threshold concept' in relation to dementia in late life

The causes of the main forms of dementia have not yet been established, but the matter is no longer shrouded in obscurity. In cases of senile dementia of Alzheimer's type for example, the hypothesis that causation is in some way closely bound up with the changes known as 'plaques', the filamentous material accummulated in the nerve cell bodies of the cortex (neurofibrillary tangles), and some other less conspicuous changes, had been shown to be consistent with the facts of observation. In the case of dementia due to multiple 'infarcts', which are areas of damage due to local circulatory blockage, the aggregation of strokes could be held responsible for the dementia. It is well known that the first one to three strokes will often be associated with transient or no intellectual impairment. Progressive deterioration sets in only after the individual has suffered a succession of strokes or a few exceptionally large ones.

The most interesting questions were posed by the senile and presenile dementias of Alzheimer's type, because it was in these disorders that the pathological changes most closely resembled those found in normal, well preserved old people. What had caused the pathological changes to become accelerated or intensified so that they outstripped what would normally be found in mentally healthy people at an advanced age?

One possibility is that senile dementia belongs to a group of disorders in which a 'threshold effect' is observed. This implies that no disability is manifest until the underlying changes develop to a certain critical point. Should they proceed beyond this point, progressive impairment in function will occur. There are some good examples of diseases of late life which appear to behave in this manner. Thus the level of glucose in the blood tends to increase with advancing age and tolerance for the glucose we consume declines. If an elderly person whose blood glucose is in the upper levels of the normal range becomes obese, he may develop the symptoms and signs of diabetes, although the change will often be reversed if he loses weight. A similar situation obtains in the case of high arterial blood pressure. And each of these conditions deal with a vicious circle in which the disease causes damage to tissues the defects of which further predispose to the disease. In the case of both of these conditions, medical science has discovered treatments that break the vicious circle in the early stage. In the case of high blood pressure this entails the use of hypotensive drugs, and in diabetes dietary measures that reduce food intake and promote weight loss.

In the case of Alzheimer's disease in its senile and presenile forms knowledge is at a more rudimentary stage of development. There is no known treatment which will arrest the dementia in its early stages. Although the 'threshold' concept is no more than an interesting hypothesis, there is a body of evidence that is consistent with it. Thus among normal people who die of accidental causes, the proportion of those in whose brains 'plaques' and 'tangles' are found at such threshold intensity increases with advancing age. Above the age of 75 years the prevalence of such changes in the brains of normal subjects goes up steeply and there is a parallel increase in the prevalence of Alzheimer's disease, which now affects the relatively high proportion of 12·5% of people.

Now if the presence of 'senile' changes in the brain really provided some kind of index of the extent to which some destructive process had been encroaching upon its reserve capacity of neurones, one would expect that the effects of other forms of brain damage would prove additive with that manifest in the 'plaques' or 'tangles'. This proves to be the case. The effects of a small amount of damage arising from strokes will in rare instances be combined with a 'senile' change or in other words, tangles and plaques. The progessive dementia that follows in such cases would not have appeared as a result of either kind of change in isolation: each kind of damage is frequently found in elderly people who die without ever exhibiting mental impairment.

The fact that a mild or moderate head injury insufficient to cause lasting intellectual deficit in a young person may be followed by dementia in an elderly one points in a similar direction. Another line of evidence is provided by the form of mental subnormality known as Down's syndrome. Dementia occurs early in this condition and is associated with abundant plaque formation.

The brain's nerve cell population is fixed at birth and those cells are incapable of subdivision. Hence the threshold concept has some important practical implications. It provides at any rate the strong suggestion that the integrity of the brain should be preserved at all stages of the lifespan, for it suggests that any damage to the brain's nerve cells will be likely to enhance the chances that dementia will develop when the individual reaches that part of the lifespan in which the concomitants of 'normal' ageing begin to make their appearance. Although the evidence is not conclusive, it would be wise to assume that protection of the brain's integrity at all stages of the lifespan will offer some measure of protection against the risk of developing dementia in old age.

Biochemical theories

In recent years the biochemical abnormalities in the brains of those with senile dementia of Alzheimer's type have attracted increasing attention. It has proved possible to investigate the activity of numerous enzymes, including those concerned with the crucial function of facilitating and controlling the passage of nerve impulses from one cell to another. A powerful impetus has been given to such studies by the successes they have achieved in the case of Parkinson's disease. Biochemical analysis of the brain regions especially concerned with the degradation of those movements which are involuntary, or undertaken outside conscious control, have demonstrated that a deficiency of one particular enzyme in those who suffer from this disease can now be remedied by administration of the compound L-dopa, bringing considerable relief to many patients who were in the past seriously incapacitated by muscular rigidity, slowness and constant tremulousness.

The dementia associated with the hereditary disease known as Huntington's Chorea has also been studied with the aid of these techniques. The enzyme, glutamic acid decarboxylase, was found to be markedly depleted in the basal ganglia of the brain of those affected. Unfortunately, this finding has not for the present led to biochemical treatments of this disorder. As far as Alzheimer's disease of senile and presenile type is concerned, observations in several centres in the United Kingdom have demonstrated a widespread deficit of the enzymes concerned with the synthesis and breakdown of the substance acetylcholine, which is intimately involved in the transmission of impulses from one neurone to the next in certain specific parts of the brain's neuronal population. The findings have been confirmed by investigators in a number of other countries.

There are certain reasons for regarding this finding as being of high promise. The deficiency is specific, being absent in other diseases such as the depressions and neuroses of old age and the dementias due to multiple strokes or other causes. In Alzheimer's disease the severity of the defect appears to correlate well with the measured number of plaques found in the brain. It is concentrated in those parts of the brain which show the most intense pathological changes. Finally, drugs such as scopolamine, which inhibit the effects of acetylcholine, produce a form of memory impairment in human subjects that bears a resemblance to that found in the early stages of dementia.

For this reason chemical treatments which could be expected to remedy the deficiencies found in Alzheimer's disease are now the subject of intensive investigation in different parts of the world. It is too early to judge the success they will achieve. There are also indications that the deficiency relating to acetylcholine may be one of a number of chemical abnormalities which interact with one another. It is, therefore, possible that pharmacological treatments will have to incorporate a number of compounds so as to compensate for all the defects identified, but the important point is that active and informative research is now being directed to the very centre of the causal process of a disease that constitutes a leading medical and social problem of our time. A mere one or two decades ago the suggestion that there might be chemical causes and chemical treatments of the commonest forms of senile and presenile dementias would have been received with incredulity.

Dementia due to an infective process

The possibility that an infective process may be at work in some of the dementias of middle and late life stems from the remarkable studies of Carleton Gajdusek into the precocious form of dementia known as 'Kuru' which is endemic among the members of the Fore tribe in New Guinea, affecting women and children of both sexes.[4] Gajdusek demonstrated that this condition could be transmitted by inoculation from the brain of a subject who had died from the disease into the brain of various species of monkeys. In a few isolated cases accidental transmissions from man to man has occurred. Gajdusek's inference from the age and sex distribution of the disorder that its causation was intimately associated in some, as yet, undetermined manner with the ritual practices of cannibalism in the tribe has received confirmation from the fact that since these practices were eradicated Kuru has ceased to afflict the tribe in question.

Some years later the rare and rapidly fatal form of dementia known as Creuzfeldt-Jakob's disease, previously attributed to brain degeneration, was also demonstrated by Gajdusek to be transmissible to chimpanzees and to New World monkeys by inoculation of brain tissue from affected patients who had died, and then the animal developed a closely similar form of brain disease. Successful transmission from one chimpanzee to another has also been achieved. Two rapidly fatal human diseases of obscure origin have, therefore, been shown in recent years to be due to an infectious organism with a long period of incubation.

The nature of the organism is, for the present, something of a scientific mystery. The usual inflammatory action generated by infectious organisms is absent from the brain, both in the animals and in the human subjects affected. The neutralising antibodies usually generated by infectious disease also fail to develop. Hence the absence of signs of infection in Alzheimer's disease and related conditions does not wholly exclude the possibility that infectious micro-organisms might contribute to their causation. As the agent that causes 'Kuru' and Creuzfeldt-Jakob disease is capable of passing extremely fine filters, it is suspected to be a virus or a minute virus-like particle similar in character to the organism that causes certain kinds of infection in plants: but it proves resistant to physical agents which would be expected to destroy all known viruses.

The disease known to veterinaries as 'Scrapie', which attacks sheep in particular, shows the same distinctive 'spongiform change' in the brain (so named because the brain appears riddled with tiny holes) as it does in Kuru and Creutzfeldt-Jakob disease. The cause is an infectious agent of a similar kind. Investigations of this disorder have shown that the incubation time in some strains may be so long that it comes close to the natural lifespan of the host. Hence, if a virus plays any part in the causation of some of the dementias of man, the infection could have begun decades before the symptoms make their appearance, possibly even in early childhood.

For the present there is no definite evidence that Alzheimer's disease of senile or presenile type is due to an infection or can be acquired through contagion from a person affected by the disease. If a viral factor in causation were firmly established it would still not become a treatable disorder overnight. However, in some preliminary experiments in the treatment of the previously incurable Creutzfeldt-Jakob disease with the antiviral agent amantadine some encouraging results were obtained in a few isolated cases, although the effect of the drug appears to have been a biochemical rather than an antiviral one.

Carleton Gajdusek was awarded a Nobel Prize in 1977 for his pioneering work on the infectious forms of dementia. Scientific investigation aimed at discovering the underlying organisms continues in his laboratory as well as in some others in different parts of the world. Scientific investigation in this field has repeatedly yielded the unexpected, and there are likely to be more surprises to come.

Dementias treatable today or tomorrow

There is a gradually expanding minority of patients with dementia due to specific causes that demand treatment with the least possible delay. The disorder may arise from hypothyroidism due to deficient secretion of the thyroid gland, or deficiency of Vitamin B_{12}, a tumour in certain parts of the brain, severe intestinal malabsorption or a large clot of blood which may form under the outer covering of the brain in old people following a relatively trivial head injury. Prompt and appropriate treatment may bring about complete recovery in such cases.

It is of interest also that the picture of dementia may arise in individuals who suffer from cancer or cancerous proliferation of the white blood cells. In some of these patients the dementia is due to the invasion by an identifiable virus of those parts of the brain which are especially concerned with memory. But there are also rare forms of brain infection due to conventional viruses such as the herpes simplex virus.

There is also a form of encephalitis which is due to a recrudescence among older children and young adults of an infection with the virus which causes measles. Most of the inflammatory diseases in the brain caused by such conventional viruses prove fatal. But about a third of those who develop encephalitis due to the virus of herpes simplex (which also causes a symptomless general infection in many people or merely gives rise to a few vesicles around the lips for a time) recover and the residual mental deficit takes the form of an impairment of short-term memory. This resembles the impairment found at an early stage in the development of senile dementia of Alzheimer's type. The prospects for patients with all such disorders would be transformed by an advance in the treatment of viral infections.

The progress of knowledge is, therefore, slowly encroaching upon a group of disorders which were regarded a few decades ago as uniformly hopeless in outcome. Scientific knowledge of Alzheimer's disease has made rapid strides in recent years and some of the experiments with treatment show great promise, though for the present this has yet to be fulfilled. But the number of treatable cases differentiated from the main body of untreatable ones is slowly but surely increasing. Some of these conditions have already been described. A further example described in recent years is a form of dementia which arises from obstruction to the free flow of the fluid which fills the ventricles of the brain and also the spaces which intervene between the surface of the brain and the coverings which separate it from the skull. The disease begins with a characteristic disorder of gait and impaired control of the sphincters, followed by a slowly developing mental impairment which begins with apathy and inattention. Relief of the obstruction will sometimes mitigate or cure the condition, particularly in younger subjects and in those who have sustained injuries to the head or have suffered haemorrhages that have given rise to a mechanical obstruction to the free flow of cerebrospinal fluid.

A rare form of dementia of obscure causation

Unexpected insights into the causes of disease are sometimes provided by investigation of rare disorders which present an exaggerated or parodied version of a common condition of unknown origin.

There is a rare disease endemic among the Chamorro peoples of the island of Guam, which gives rise either to a combination of mental deterioration with Parkinsonism or to a characteristic type of progressive muscular wasting. It occurs in identical form in many parts of the world. This rare condition is of great interest from a scientific point of view for a number of reasons. It causes premature death in early or middle life in a relatively high proportion of men on the island. About one in five deaths over the age of 25 on the Island of Guam result from it. Hereditary factors may contribute, but it has not so far proved possible to establish decisively the operation of a genetic factor. One of the most interesting facts about this disorder is that two of the pathological changes found in the brain after death are identical in appearance and ultra-microscopic character to two of the changes typical of Alzheimer's disease of senile and presenile type.

Moreover, the brain of a substantial minority of well-preserved Chamorros proved to have similar changes in their brain in attenuated form without their showing any mental or neurological symptoms or signs. However, in contrast to the form of change known as the 'plaque', commonly found in the brain of well-preserved elderly Caucasian subjects, middle-aged and elderly subjects on the islands of Guam and also some Japanese are found to exhibit 'neurofibrillary tangles', a form of change which is virtually never found in the cerebral cortex in large numbers among old people in the West except in cases of indubitable dementia of Alzheimer's type. Hence, as far as the most conspicuous structural changes found in the ageing brain are concerned, there is no one type of cerebral structural alteration that proves to hold for all members of the human species. There is a certain amount of variation between different ethnic groups.

However, there is enough overlap in the character of the changes in Alzheimer's disease and Guam Parkinsonism dementia to make it likely that any advances in knowledge in respect of the latter would shed light also on the most widely prevalent forms of dementia in the world. The Guam Syndrome seems to be a particularly strong candidate for discovery of specific causes and, although a number of ideas regarding causation have already been investigated without definite results, there is ample scope for further investigation with the aid of the more refined chemical and structural techniques brought to bear in recent years in the investigation of senile and other forms of dementia in the countries of the West.

Future perspectives

A confluence of new evidence from clinical observation, classical neuropathology, ultra-microscopy, neurochemistry and the lessons derived from certain specific models of dementia such as in Kuru, Creutzfeldt-Jakob disease and the cluster of neuropsychiatric disorders indigenous in the island of Guam have created a climate of high promise for the scientific investigation of dementia.[5] The prospects both for clinical and scientific work have been greatly enhanced by a number of important recent technical advances. The CAT (Computerised Axial Tomography) scan provides a picture of the detailed regional structure of the human brain by a technique a hundred times more sensitive than conventional x-rays. Moreover, unlike the methods available in the past, this new type of x-ray examination is simple and entirely safe and can be undertaken without anaesthesia or invasive procedures. Further, the pioneering studies of Lassen and Ingvar on the investigation of the blood flow of the human brain have been carried to a further stage by the recently introduced techniques of Dr Sokoloff of Washington. This entails an intravenous injection of a radioactive analogue of glucose and makes it possible to study the metabolism of different regions of the human brain in detail. This highly sensitive technique has transformed the prospects for identifying the early stages of senile and other forms of dementia and will open up enquiries in other directions.

Neurochemistry deserves special mention here, because in the past six to seven years a relatively new science has emerged with the demonstration that the chemistry of the human brain and substances which mediate transmission along different neuronal pathways in particular, can be investigated after death. In the past it had been assumed that the decomposition which is set in motion by death would make it impossible to shed light on brain chemistry by this method. The fact that this assumption has proved to be in error and that it has been found possible to shed light on the chemistry of neurotransmitters and other substances in the brain and to correlate the findings with measures of structural change and with observations on psychological function and diagnosis recorded during life, represents an important step forward.[6]

Some of the results that have accrued within this short period of time have led workers on ageing to revise firmly ingrained ideas. It has, in the past, been assumed that the intellectual deterioration that was manifest in dementia (and to a more limited extent in the course of normal ageing) stems from the progressive and generalised death and outfall of brain cells which, once lost, could not be replaced. But it is less certain now whether generalised loss of neurones occurs. The earliest mental changes do not necessarily derive from cellular destruction. And the situation regarding death and outfall of cells in senile dementia proves to be more complicated than had been previously envisaged. This can be summarised by making the point that the death of cells appears to be highly selective, affecting those in which the impulses are mediated by one kind of transmitter while leaving others intact.

It has proved possible to investigate the concentration in the brain of many chemical substances concerned with neuronal activity, including a number which are known to be located within the cell bodies of intrinsic neurones of the cerebral cortex and those which are not within the cells. The substance somatostatin is an example of the former and cholecystokinin of the latter. These investigations suggest that certain populations of cells probably fall out, being reduced by as much as 50%, while others appear entirely intact, as indicated by the normal concentration of the chemical substances located within them. Quite recently, investigations in Cambridge and Newcastle have demonstrated that one nucleus within the brain may suffer a loss of as many as 80% of its cell population in forms of dementia that commence at a relatively early age. This nucleus gives rise to neurones in which the transmitter is nor-epinephrine. In a chemical and structural sense the problem is complex and the full picture remains to be unravelled. It looks as if a number of biochemical deficits may need to be compensated for if future treatments of dementia are to have any hope of success. Be this as it may, the situation will be basically no different from that which has materialised in the case of Parkinsonism, where the biochemical deficit has proved to be susceptible of correction up to a certain point with the aid of drugs. This is the prospect of highest promise which has been opened up in the enquiries of the past quarter of a century. The hopes of those engaged in working in this field represent the dreams and fantasies men have cherished down the ages of being able to defeat the effects of ageing. If these hopes have not yet been fulfilled, they have at least been shown not to have been wholly without substance, and as senile dementia is, in many respects, a parody of old age, any advances in the knowledge of its causation are bound to have some implications for prevention and treatment. Perhaps it is in the brain that the programme which predestines the duration of a lifespan and the character of the ageing process that precedes death is encoded, running out like the tape recording of a Beethoven symphony when the relevant neuronal structures undergo destruction.

This chapter has been largely devoted to the subject of dementia. Perhaps a corrective should be added to draw attention once again to the advances already made in the mitigation of many other forms of mental suffering in old age. The distress of large numbers of old people who have been affected in the past by states of severe depression and anxiety, obsessions and phobias, and who have suffered for years on end without hope of relief, can now be mitigated and at times wholly banished. We now recognise these conditions as merely coloured by the qualities of old age, not determined by the process of ageing as such. The same statement can be made for many of those tormented by delusions of persecution. But there is one fact above all which motivates those who investigate the problems of dementia in the aged. This is the enormous disparity between those who go into their eighties and nineties with minds undimmed and those who are already demented in their seventies or even at a much earlier age. There must be explanations for these disparities and it does not seem fanciful or unrealistic to look to science for the narrowing of this gap. The life of a Bertrand Russell who, after leading a long, stormy and productive life, can die relatively intact at 98, having continued to work almost until the end, provides the inspiration for a working philosophy towards problems of ageing which has been expressed elsewhere by Sir Martin Roth:

> 'The wise, humane psychiatrist will work on the assumption that activity, stimulus and challenge help to preserve the mind, and surviving human relation-

ships keep the emotions alive, and that the sense of purpose or the quest for it conserves the personality. . . .'

Those who are engaged in the clinical practice of mental disorder in old age continue to give expression to such tentative theories in their every day work even though scientific evidence for them is tenuous.

References

1. Eisdorfer C., Fann W. E. (1982). *Treatment of Psychology in Ageing*. New York: Springer.
2. Murphy E. (1983). Prognosis of depression in old age. *Brit. J. Psychiat*; **142**: 111–9.
3. Pitt B. (1983). *Psychogeriatrics: an Introduction to the Psychiatry of Old Age*. 2nd edn. Edinburgh: Churchill Livingtone.
4. Gajdusek D. C., Gibbs J. C. (1975). Slow virus infections of the nervous system and the laboratories of slow, latent temperate virus infections. In *The Nervous System*, Vol. 2 (Tower D. B., ed.) pp. 113–35. New York: Raven Press.
5. Roth M. (1980). Perspectives in the scientific study of mental illness in old age. In *Priorities in Psychiatric Research* (Lader M., ed.) pp. 91–116. Chichester: John Wiley.
6. Emson P. C., Lindvall O. (1979). Distribution of putative neuro-transmitters in the neocortex. *Neuroscience*; **4**: 1–30.

13
Research in Forensic Psychiatry

There are few more intractable problems than those concerned with violence, vandalism, rape and similar criminal offences. What can be done to reduce the crime and antisocial behaviour in the country, and how can criminals be induced to mend their ways? There have always been those who call for heavier punishments and stricter application of the law. It is now recognised, however, that there are other factors, including social attitudes and the mental state of the offenders, which play a part in criminal behaviour but which are not influenced by punishment. Among those brought to trial, there are some who are mentally handicapped or mentally sick and others who are young and immature. Here, therefore, is an area in which psychiatrists are able to help. Their assistance is called for, not only in the diagnosis of mental abnormalities in offenders, but also in giving advice on their treatment and on their disposal. Should they be sent to prison, to an institution such as a mental hospital, or to a Borstal centre? The efficient operation of the courts of law is clearly essential in order to maintain law and order and thus to safeguard the general welfare of the community. But experience has shown the need also for preventive measures based on an understanding of the mental attitudes current in different sections of the community, including various sectarian organisations and ethnic groups. Here again, psychiatry has its part to play, not only in individual cases, but also in situations as, for example, the riots that have erupted in our cities and universities.

Both in the criminal and civil courts problems frequently arise in the solution of which lawyers turn increasingly to the psychiatrists for help. In criminal cases the psychiatrist may be asked to examine the accused person and to give expert advice in court on the nature of his mental disorder, the extent of his responsibility and the prospects for treatment either in hospital or in the community. In civil proceedings the psychiatrist may be asked to advise on questions arising in connection with the family, such as care-orders, custody of the children, marital disputes, divorce or adoption. His help may be sought in connection with conflicts over compensation, or the law applicable to the noncriminal mentally ill, or the mentally handicapped.

Criminal responsibility

It is a characteristic feature of the Anglo-Saxon legal systems, particularly in relation to serious crimes, that consideration is given to the mental state of the offender in determining his liability to punishment. An individual is excused the liability to punishment if at the time of carrying out a forbidden act he was mentally disordered, unconscious, mistaken or, in some cases, if he was acting under threat or some form of duress. If his mental state was not such that his behaviour could be completely excused, it could be accepted that his responsibility for the forbidden act was diminished, and that would be reflected in a reduced sentence. The concept of reduced legal responsibility has arisen from a number of different considerations including current views on morality and justice. Other Anglo-Saxon systems of law have been strongly influenced by the British approach, the historical development of which has been skilfully traced by Professor Nigel Walker of the Cambridge Institute of Criminology in his outstanding study.[1]

Opinions on criminal responsibility have been changing in recent years. Some, such as Lady Wootton, have regarded the reliance on the mental state of the defendant (*mens rea*) in determining whether an offence was committed as illogical and incapable of proof, but others have considered it irrational to omit any mention of the intention to commit a crime from all aspects of the criminal law. However, an increasing number of crimes are now regarded as offences of strict liability only, requiring no element of intent for guilt to be established and this represents a departure from the older principles of liberty and justice. The long-established McNaughton Rules (1843) laid down that an accused person could escape responsibility for a criminal act only if he was labouring under such *'a defect of reason, from disease of the mind, as not to know the nature and quality of the act, or if he did know it, not to know that what he was doing was wrong'*. But these rules are now rarely used. The Homicide Act of 1957 introduced the notion of diminished responsibility, which provided a more flexible approach by allowing a mentally abnormal individual charged with murder to plead guilty to the lesser offence of manslaughter. If this is accepted, it allows the Judge freedom to award a sentence more appropriate than life imprisonment, the fixed sentence for murder. In the past 23 years almost all mentally abnormal murderers have been dealt with as cases of diminished responsibility, although about 40% have received a prison sentence, sometimes life imprisonment.

The Butler Committee on Mentally Abnormal Offenders (1975) sought to establish a new form of 'special verdict' that would be more relevant in cases of this kind—*'not guilty on evidence of mental disorder'*. This would exempt from conviction not only those who did not know what they were doing, but also those defendants suffering from 'severe mental illness' or 'severe subnormality'. The new verdict could be returned in a magistrate's court as well as in a Crown Court, and either would have the power to decide on the appropriate disposal of the offender. At present the offender must be sent to a hospital, which may be a Special Hospital. Other proposals that have been made include changes in the laws relating to diminished responsibility, infanticide, automatism and offences committed under the influence of alcohol. Other recommendations of the Butler Committee have been modified by the

Criminal Law Revision Committee, but their further consideration awaits the necessary allocation of parliamentary time. The complex problems arising from the notion of diminished responsibility have benefited mainly from research based on the statistical and descriptive analysis of defences relying on psychiatric evidence that have been used by the courts over the years.

Treatment of offenders

The specialist services that are needed for the accommodation and treatment of mentally disordered offenders depend on the nature and the prevalence of psychiatric disorders in the criminal population. Interest in this need began in the mid-ninteenth century as a result of the work of Dr J. Bruce Thomson, First Medical Officer of Perth prison in Scotland, who carried out surveys of the mental and physical health of prisoners under his care. Dr Charles Goring, Medical Officer, conducted similar surveys at Parkhurst prison which tended to refute the earlier work of Lombroso, the Italian criminologist, who had suggested that biological causative factors were of primary importance in determining criminal behaviour. The work of Sir Norwood East and his collaborator Dr W. Hubert, published in 1939, is an important landmark in this field of research. They studied a selected group of 406 prisoners at Wormwood Scrubbs prison who had been individually referred from other prisons as cases that might benefit from psychiatric treatment. Most were sex offenders, some were arsonists and others had committed crimes considered to be due to obsessional or hysterical reactions or 'some other remediable condition'. The report resulting from this research recommended the establishment of a specialised psychiatric prison within the system, which led ultimately to the opening of Grendon Underwood prison in 1964. Grendon represents the most imaginative experiment in treatment that the prison system in the UK has attempted in the past fifty years, and its development has been observed with interest by its supporters and critics alike.

Gunn and his colleagues[2] have studied the effect on prisoners of the Grendon regime which is based on group methods, the development of self-responsibility and the encouragement of mutual respect and trust. They have shown that the success of Grendon is demonstrable in the improvement in the attitude of the prisoners to authority and in their improved outlook rather than in the effect on their reconviction rate. The Grendon approach is a more positive and humanitarian one than that of the traditional regime of conventional prisons.

In recent years prisons have received an increasing number of mentally disturbed individuals, of whom some should be receiving hospital care. Bluglass[3] examined one in four of all admissions to Perth Prison and found that 46% presented psychiatric problems of one kind or another. This group included 11% who had a significant alcohol or drug problem, 12% who were 'borderline subnormal', and 13% who were given a diagnosis of 'psychopathic personality'. A similar study of the prison population in the South East of England suggested that 35% were 'psychiatric cases'. The proportion of mentally abnormal prisoners has tended to rise since these studies were carried out, so increasing the need to plan alternative facilities for their care within the National Health Service.

Professor Gibbens and his collaborators assessed the use of the remand for a psychiatric report by magistrates in all the Inner London magistrates courts and in the area administered by the Wessex Regional Health Authority.[4] About 1–2% of all offenders appearing before the courts were remanded for a psychiatric report, but there were marked differences in the two areas. For the same offence and with a similar background an offender in Wessex was more likely to be remanded on bail and to receive a recommendation for probation or treatment. The research results reflected the better services and treatment facilities in Wessex where more psychiatrists are involved in assessment and where they have developed good relationships with the Probation Services. During the past decade forensic psychiatry services have been developing within the National Health Service in different parts of the country, and in some areas regional psychiatric intensive care units (regional secure units) are also being established. The work described above has made an important contribution to these advances and there is now a need for further research to monitor the progress of the secure unit programme and the operation of the units themselves. Similarly, the populations of the Special Hospitals provide valuable opportunities for research and they have already been the subject of a number of useful studies. A Special Hospital Research Unit now coordinates these activities in the UK. A forensic psychiatry research group based on the Department of Health also promotes operational research in the National Health Service.

Violence and aggression

Research in recent years which has increased our understanding of the causes of delinquency includes an important survey by teacher and parent questionnaires and by interview, of some 2000 adolescents aged 14–15 on the Isle of Wight.[5] West, who studied the development of 400 London boys from the age of 8–16, studied the onset and course of delinquent behaviour and related it to their social circumstances, ability, performance and family background. In a thirty-year follow-up of 524 children seen originally in a Child Guidance clinic, Professor Lee Robins of the Washington University School of Medicine compared their adult status with that of 100 normal control subjects.

She found that a high proportion of those who had attended the Child Guidance clinic (45%) had developed adult antisocial behaviour, and a slightly higher proportion than in the control subjects had developed schizophrenia, alcoholism, hysteria or chronic brain syndrome. These studies have all added significantly to our knowledge of the development of adult delinquency. Important studies of Borstal inmates and of girls admitted to approved schools have added further to our understanding of delinquency in the adolescent age group.

A different approach to the study of aggression and of other specific types of behaviour has been made in recent years in animal studies of the higher primates and particularly of chimpanzees. The observations of aggressive behaviour in natural habitats and in captive colonies, and of patterns of learning and adaptation, have also suggested possible lines of enquiry in man. Of particular interest is the evidence of the influence of hormones on the early development of the brain and their relationship to subsequent aggressive behaviour.

There is a continual search for a greater understanding of the origins of violent behaviour, the biological and social factors that influence it, the predictive signs of future dangerous behaviour and for better methods of modification and management. Murder cases have been studied intensively with reference to the incidence of psychiatric illness, the value of the electro-encephalogram in diagnosis and the relevance of factors such as suicide, drugs, alcohol, special syndromes (such as morbid jealousy) and epilepsy.[6] Non-accidental injury to children has been a special focus of research interest during the past decade. This has involved studies of the parents of battered children, of the psychopathology of the families and of methods of identification, reporting and prevention all of which have resulted in improved understanding of the causes and the better organisation of services to cope with the cases that arise.[7] This research has led to a wider awareness of other forms of violence in the family, directed, for example, against wives (battered wives), and more recently of violence directed against the dependent elderly.

Research leading into the origins of violent behaviour, whether occurring between individuals or large groups in the community acting together, has received an impetus as a result of the increasing evidence of aggressive and destructive activity in the world at large. In addition to studies relating to biological and social influences, research derived from learning theory and from chromosomal analysis has made a contribution. Long-term studies of criminal careers, of crowd behaviour, and of the influence of television, the cinema and literature have also helped.

Other investigations have concentrated on studies of specific groups of aggressive or destructive offenders such as arsonists, thieves, dangerous drivers or rapists. The need to seek ways of preventing and controlling violence is linked with the attempt to identify accurate methods of predicting future dangerous behaviour, which is one of the most important functions of those who have the task of either sentencing or returning violent individuals to the community. Studies of personality types have also contributed to our understanding of the problem, but have increasingly suggested that the concept of 'psychopathic personality' as a specific category of mental disorder characterised by an identifiable natural history is over-simplistic and unhelpful.

Sexually deviant offenders, although a relatively small proportion of all criminals, frequently pose difficult therapeutic problems for the psychiatrist. In recent years there has been a greater effort to understand the aetiology of sexual behaviour, made possible by a more tolerant and less inhibited social climate. Our approach remains based to a considerable extent upon hypotheses derived from psychoanalytic and behavioural models, but advances have been made from studies of genetic factors, from studies of twins, and from investigations of the influence of hormones. Studies of parent and child relationships and of social learning in animals and man have also added to our knowledge, but despite this our knowledge remains limited. There have been many studies of homosexuality and a number of investigations of specific behaviour such as exhibitionism (indecent exposure), transsexualism and transvestism, incest, sexual violence and paedophilia. Some studies are of individual cases analysed in depth while others are follow-up studies of groups of cases tracing future behaviour. Other research relates to the influence of the family, the long-term effects of violence on victims or the results of various different treatment approaches. However our knowledge of the factors that determine sexual identity, sexual behaviour and sexual preference remains poor, but, the successful results of treatment in some individual cases by psychotherapy, group or behaviour therapy, hormones or antilibidinal drugs encourages the search for more basic information on causation and the effects of treatment.

Some specific offences have been the subject of special study. Professor Gibbens' survey and follow-up of shoplifters in London drew attention to a particular group, mainly women, who steal for psychological reasons rather than for motives of need or greed. They are often mentally disturbed and they benefit from treatment. This work has had an important influence on the approach of the courts, but there is still a need for further research into this problem. There have been other specific studies of vagrants, drug addicts and alcoholics, all of them of importance in relation to the problem of crime in general, its control and the provision of services.

Besides the problems that have been mentioned, there is a very real need for a greater understanding of the causes of violence, not only within the bounds of national communities, but also at an international level. International disputes and wars are commonly attributed to impersonal economic, social or historical factors. However, recent research into the causes of war has drawn attention to the part played by individuals of high responsibility in key positions, whose powers of good judgement and decision-making at critical periods are now known to have been seriously affected in some cases by factors such as advancing age, personality defects, undue stress, and even by alcohol, drugs and by physical disease.[8] In the present nuclear age we are more than ever dependent on the maintenance of international law and to this end further forensic research might prove to be of value. While research in the field of forensic psychiatry has made an important contribution to our understanding of human behaviour, precise knowledge is still sadly very limited and treatment remains in the main empirical. Although the clinical approach should not be undervalued, there is still much that can be done by forensic psychiatrists trained to investigate these complex problems using the tools of modern scientific research.

References

1. Walker N. (1968). *Crime and Insanity in England*. Edinburgh: University Press.
2. Gunn J., Robertson G., Dell S., Way C. (1978). *Psychiatric Aspects of Imprisonment*. London: Academic Press.
3. Bluglass R. (1966). *A Psychiatric Study of Scottish Convicted Prisoners*. MD Thesis. University of St Andrews.
4. Gibbens, T. C. N., Soothill K. L., Pope P. J. (1977). *Medical Remands in Criminal Courts*. Oxford: Oxford University Press.
5. Graham P., Rutter M. (1973). Psychiatric disorder in the young adolescent; a follow-up study. *Proc. Roy. Soc. Med*; **66**: 1226–9.
6. Bluglass R. (1979). The psychiatric assessment of homicide *Brit. J. Hosp. Med*; **21**: 366–77.
7. Franklin A. W., ed (1975). *Concerning Child Abuse*. London: Churchill Livingstone.
8. L'Etang H. (1980). *Fit to Lead?* London: Heinemann Medical.

14
Research in Community Care

'Community Care' is a concept that has led to much controversy amongst both professionals and the lay public in recent years—not least as to just what it means.

Fundamentally, though, it stems from the view that patients with psychiatric disorders do not in general need to be treated now within institutions which have a primary function of segregation from the general community. As early as 1953, an expert committee of the World Health Organization contrasted the 'classical' system of care, founded on the mental hospital, with a modern system that makes use of a variety of different institutions and community services. Whilst a policy of making relatively less use of hospital care was favoured by the majority of both professional staff and the general public, the community approach was not concerned only with where this care took place. It was also an expression of contemporary feelings in society that people in general have a right to self-determination and control over many of the forces that affect them. In that case, they should have some power of selection as to the kind of treatment or care they may receive when suffering from psychiatric disorder. It should not be just a matter of admission to the mental hospital or nothing.

The distinguished British social psychiatrist Dr Douglas Bennett has emphasised that community psychiatry must be grounded on the relationship of social factors to psychiatric illness. It must aim to be concerned, not just with those who are defined at any time as 'patients', but with the psychiatric health of the whole population (e.g. of a town or district) over a significant period of time. Whereas community care began in Britain as an attempt to provide treatment outside the mental hospitals for the kind of patients who had been treated in such institutions in the past, it later became embodied in a national plan to provide comprehensive district-based mental health services. It was hoped that these would consist everywhere of psychiatric units in general hospitals, acting in a complementary way with local authority social service departments. However, although general hospital psychiatric units have grown to the extent that they now cover about a quarter of all psychiatric admissions in England and Wales, and although the total number of occupied beds in mental hospitals has fallen steadily, the trend towards the phasing out of mental hospitals has slowed down drastically, mainly because of the enormous expense involved.

Whilst 'community care' is a term that has had many meanings, Rehin and Martin proposed reasonably that it could be applied to any scheme that provided extramural care and treatment, that facilitated early detection of illness and its informal treatment, and that provided social services for the mentally ill in the general community. Thus, it has been useful as a guiding principle, even if this has at times been oversimplified. Amongst the advantages of community psychiatry are its ability to serve a broader clientèle than the old-style mental hospital, its greater visibility to public scrutiny than an isolated institution, and the fact that patients' homes and families help to make up for deficiencies in the services.[1]

Much progress appears to have been achieved towards the widely accepted aim of providing a community-based service, but two fundamental questions remain to be fully answered. Firstly, what should 'community care' mean in actual practice (e.g. hostels, day centres, counselling, voluntary help, family care)? Secondly, if such a pattern were achieved, to what extent would it result in better mental health for the population as a whole? In the end, that is the only valid objective of any such developments, but the problems which arise when attempts are made to answer these questions scientifically are formidable indeed. At the same time, it should be remembered that classical mental hospital care has never been evaluated in such a scrupulous way.

The impetus to avoid prolonged stay in hospital, which often resulted formerly in the psychiatrically ill spending most of their adult lives in institutions, arose out of an awareness of the changes which occur in people because of institutionalisation. These are loss of drive, loss of personal identity and often dignity, as well as a shrinking of abilities even beyond the damage that the original illness had caused. In our present society, such a process is universally decried, and many institutions have responded by improving the social atmosphere of ward life so as to provide greater stimulation and individual choice. There may be more subtle ways than gross institutionalisation, however, in which admission to hospital adversely affects the mentally ill person. Taking on the identity of the sick person, he may persist in this role even after his acute symptoms have disappeared, and may shrink from personal responsibilities that he would otherwise be able to master. He may become estranged from his family, or at least lose his role in that family ('father', 'breadwinner', etc.) and this may further diminish self-esteem. It is sometimes argued that hospitalisation aids the process by which some disturbed families may scapegoat one member, wrongly blaming the disturbance on that member, rather than on the family relationships.

To weigh the benefits to the patient and 'the community' (usually his family) of the patient remaining out of hospital for much or all of his illness, and to compare these benefits with the drawbacks and strain of the arrangement, poses a challenge to the researcher. Preventing hospitalisation, indeed closing down the mental hospitals, may seem so right on moral grounds alone in our present society that we may be blind to the pitfalls. The most obvious pitfall is that the family may simply not be able to cope, and may itself suffer damage.

Research in this area was pioneered in Britain. Grad and Sainsbury, of the Medical Research Council, in the early 1960s used the term 'family burden'. They assessed the ways in which patients affected their households, and measured the extent of this effect through a Family Burden Scale, which categorised disruptions of the household in terms of work, school, leisure, domestic routine, etc. Hoenig and Hamilton in the North West similarly examined two newly developed services based on general hospitals; the family members interviewed there with specially devised questions gave clear evidence of the objective burden to the family in respect of loss of earnings, poor health and stressful behaviour by the patient, such as restlessness or wandering. In some cases, a wish was expressed that more could be done by the statutory services, but the burning issue was whether the new type of service would lead to a higher overall strain on families than the traditional service, based on prolonged hospitalisation.

A difficulty in assessing that issue is that of finding two services where the range and severity of illness are sufficiently similar, so that any differences in, say, family burden can be attributed to the different nature of the services, rather than the differing types or severity of the illnesses of the patients being treated. An experiment is the best research approach to this, but requires a fairly typical and broad range of patients, in which the results of admission to a short-stay programme could be compared with a more traditional form of treatment. Kennedy and Hird's study in Edinburgh, conducted in 1977, and funded by a voluntary source, the Mental Health Foundation, achieved a satisfactory distinction between short and longer stay. Acutely ill patients who were deemed to require admission to a Psychiatric Hospital, could either be admitted to the experimental service or to the traditional wards. Random allocation prevented a bias towards one type of service receiving more severely ill patients than the other.

The policy was that hospital stay in the experimental ward should be as brief as possible, though whenever necessary, a patient might remain in hospital for longer. The average length of stay in the experimental ward (17 days) was half that of the traditional wards. In the experimental programme, decisions about treatment were taken as quickly as possible; nurses rather than doctors were more actively involved than in traditional wards, and were often responsible for outpatient follow-ups; and the patients were frequently offered treatment as day patients (attending the ward from 9 a.m. to 5 p.m.). All programmes provided daily group therapy and occupational therapy, whilst drugs and occasionally ECT for severe depression were used as required.

The short-stay group were as well as the longer stay group at follow-up 3 weeks and 4 months after discharge; they reached that level after a shorter total time than the longer stay group. With respect to psychiatric symptoms, the only difference between the groups during the follow-up periods was that suicide attempts were more common in the longer stay group. Role performance (ability to perform duties at home and at work) was improving in the short-stay patients at the 4 month follow-up, but diminishing in the longer stay patients at the equivalent time after discharge. Thus, not only were the short-stay patients doing better from the point of view of symptoms, but the family might have been expected to be benefiting from their better role performance. A similar study in London reached the same conclusion. Was this reduction of hospitalisation at the expense, however, of stress in the family? Ratings of family burden obtained from interviews with relatives or friends at the two points after discharge did not show up any difference in family burden between the two groups. The doubt which lingers a little here is whether the research interview was a sufficiently sensitive thermometer of family burden to have detected a difference between the groups. Indeed, work continues on devising ways of assessing family stress so that we can be sure that the vital question about whether 'the community' can cope is properly answered.

One of the best attempts so far to assess the value of a community-based alternative to care in mental hospitals has come from a major research programme carried out in Wisconsin over a number of years by Stein and Test. The alternative model involves minimal use of the hospital, much direct intervention by the service in patients' homes, and giving support to affected members of the community as well as to the patients themselves. Patients who were cared for along these lines over a period of 14 months were compared with controls, treated in a mental hospital for as long as necessary, and then referred to a community agency. Each group consisted of a number of unselected patients, applying for admission to a mental hospital.

Throughout the experimental period almost all the subjects of the special community programme were able to remain out of hospital, and this was not at the expense of their quality of life or self-esteem. Indeed, compared with the control patients, experimental subjects showed better functioning in several significant respects, less subjective distress and greater satisfaction with their lives. However, when the special treatment programme was stopped, the differences between the two groups tended to get steadily less. Therefore, it seemed that for many chronically disabled psychiatric patients, community treatment should be a comprehensive and continuous effort, if they are to be maintained for long in community life.

When the burdens placed by patients on their families were assessed by the Family Burden Scale, there was no evidence that the experimental approach caused more stress on the family or community than did the traditional approach. However, the community treatment programme provided an enormous amount of support to patients, families and community members. This seemed to be the crucial element in effective community care, and the question has to be asked, to what extent would it be possible to supply a service of this intensity throughout any country? Nevertheless, Stein and Test do appear to have shown that if the effort is strong enough, then the results are impressive.

Another aspect of this question is that of cost, however. On the whole, it is cheaper to fund 'community care' than to build hospitals. Developing countries have been interested in the model of Aro village in Nigeria, where the local community, as well as the patients' families, are actively involved in treatment and rehabilitation, thereby avoiding expansion of the mental hospitals. In industrial countries, though, the situation is different and it remains to be shown whether good community care involving special treatment will turn out to be actually cheaper than the earlier model of hospital-based services. A cost-benefit study of the community-treatment service in Wisconsin showed that, in comparison with mental hospital treatment, the additional benefits it provided greatly outweighed the additional costs.

In Montreal, a controlled comparison was made between two groups of patients, most of whom were fairly young and suffering from schizophrenic or manic-depressive psychosis. They were matched for all important characteristics, and then randomly assigned to either hospital-based care or community-based home care. Follow-up reviews were then carried out at intervals for up to a year. Hospitalisation was either prevented altogether or minimised in 92% of the Home Care patients; most of the Hospital Care patients spent their first month in hospital. During the first three months, Home Care patients received much more outpatient treatment than Hospital Care patients, but then this trend was reversed for the rest of the year, with Hospital Care patients having much more outpatient attention. It was concluded that community-based care of this kind is an effective alternative to hospital-based care for many severely disabled patients.

In the UK an important contribution to community care is now being made by voluntary organisations of various different kinds. Local associations of Hospital Friends attached to the mental hospitals arrange activities such as the visiting of friendless patients and the running of social clubs which help the patient to maintain contact with members of the community. A number of charitable organisations have now arranged the establishment and running of hostels and group homes which provide sheltered accommodation for patients who may be well enough to live and work in the community, but who are unable to return to their homes. There are also several national organisations which are helping to relieve the burden on the families of mental patients by providing them with information and arranging meetings at which the relatives of mental patients can meet and discuss their problems. Active in this respect are MIND, the National Schizophrenic Fellowship, the Schizophrenia Association the Samaritans and the Alzheimer's Disease Society, while other organisations such as Alcoholics Anonymous and Turning Point are helping with the treatment of patients with problems of alcoholism and drug addiction. An important aspect of community care is the education of the general public, and this has been helped by the publications that some of the voluntary organisations have produced.[2,3,4] They have also assisted by raising funds for pioneering projects and for research. The Mental Health Foundation and the Wellcome Trust have supported a number of worthwhile research investigations and by giving Research Fellowships they have encouraged a number of promising younger clinicians to enter the field of psychiatric research. More recently, the Royal College of Psychiatrists has developed a programme of research in mental disorders and it has been giving advice to clinicians on problems relating to research.

One of the characteristics of community care in the UK is the manner in which it has been developed, largely unstandardised, and often depending on the efforts of enthusiastic individuals. As a result of this the character of the service in one area may be totally different from that in an adjacent area. For instance, within a single hospital one psychiatrist may be running a crisis intervention service operating on the flying squad principle, while his colleagues engage in conventional hospital-based practice. This uneven development provides the opportunity to carry out naturalistic studies comparing one type of service with another. Unfortunately, these opportunities for research have hardly ever been exploited, largely because of the difficulties involved in evaluating a total service. As can be seen from the studies quoted above, it is necessary to pay attention to the relatives as well as to the patients. Since one of the principles of community care is the provision of a comprehensive service, it is necessary to enquire whether patients of all ages and with the whole range of psychiatric conditions are being cared for adequately. Furthermore, it is not sufficient to confine the enquiry to the patients' symptoms: attention must be paid to their social needs, including accommodation, occupation, the social support available, and that elusive but all-important entity, the quality of life. The prospect of including measures of all these factors in a single study is daunting, but research of this kind must be tackled so that community care can develop in a more rational way than has been the case to date.

While the general trend today is to maintain as many patients as possible in the community, since the outcome is generally better when a patient is cared for in a community setting, research is needed to determine which kinds of patients are most successfully managed in a hospital or a hostel setting and which do best in their homes.[5] Here again, further information is needed on the conditions within the family which contribute to or which detract from success. It is clear that community care is a developing field that could benefit greatly from the guidance and understanding that could be obtained by further research.

References

1. Bowman E. P., Shelley R. K., Sheehy-Skeffington A., Sinanan K. (1983). Day patient versus in-patient: factors determining selection of acutely ill patients for hospital treatment. *Brit. J. Psychiat*; **142**: 584–7.
2. Meacher M., ed (1979). *New Methods of Mental Health Care*. Oxford: Pergamon Press.
3. Rollin H. R., ed (1980). *Coping with Schizophrenia*. London: Burnett Books/André Deutsch.
4. Mental Health Foundation (1980). *Pioneering Community Mental Health Services*. London: Mental Health Foundation.
5. Sainsbury P. (1980). In *Priorities in Psychiatric Research* (Lader M., ed.). Chichester: John Wiley.

Index

Acetylcholine 143
Adoption studies 103
Adoptive children 12
Adult delinquency 158
Affective disorders 50, 61
Age effects. *See* Old age
Aggressive behaviour 158–61
Agoraphobia 20, 32
Alcohol consumption levels 36–37
  safe 38
Alcoholics Anonymous 46, 170
Alcoholism and alcohol-related problems 35–47, 161, 170
  abstinence concept 46
  and suicide 49, 55
  at-risk factors 40
  at-risk occupations 43
  causes of 43–45
  components of 35
  controlled drinking 46
  current views of 35
  dependence syndrome 38, 39
  effect of national culture 43
  effect on brain 42
  effect on fetus 42–43
  efficacy of treatment 45–47
  genetic factors 44
  incidence of 3
  increase in 36
  intensive inpatient treatment 46
  myths relating to 46
  personality features 45
  physical problems 39
  political implications of research 36–38
  predisposing factors 44
  problems associated with excessive drinking 38–43
  psychological problems 39
  social problems 39
  traditional views of 35
  universal alcoholic personality 44
  withdrawal symptoms 38
  withdrawal syndrome 45
Alzheimer's disease 139–48
Alzheimer's Disease Society 170
Amine break-down products 60
Amino acids 129
Amitriptyline 16
Amphetamine 60, 80
Amphetamine psychosis 99
Anorexia nervosa 4
Antidepressant drugs 16, 18, 29, 55, 60, 64, 66

Antipsychotic drugs 6, 10, 11, 90
Anxiety during exposure 24
Anxiety disorder 14
Anxiety effects 22, 23, 29, 77, 107, 137
Anxiety states 16
Arteriosclerotic dementia 4
Ativan 17
Attempted suicide. *See* Suicide attempts

Barbiturates 17, 49, 55
Battered children 159
Battered wives 159
Behaviour therapy 79
Behavioural disorders in children 107
Behavioural problems 79
Behavioural psychotherapy 19–24
Benzodiazepines 17
Bereavement 16, 50, 54, 59
Biological factors 15
Blood flow 149
Blood levels 67
Blood pressure 140
Blood test 71
Bolvidon 18
Brain, effect of alcohol abuse 42
Brain development 126
Brain function 11
Brain scan 82
Brain scarring 106
Brain shrinkage 42, 82
Brain structure 80, 82
  changes in 100–2, 138–39, 145, 147–48
Butler Committee on Mentally Abnormal Offenders 155
Butobarbitone 17
Butyrophenones 81

Catego computer programme 87, 88
Central nervous system, antenatal and postnatal infections of 124
Cerebrospinal fluid 104
Chamorro peoples 147
Changing conditions in society 1
Chichester Community Psychiatric Service 58
Child abuse 114–17, 159
Child care 12
Child development 121
Child Guidance clinics 107, 112, 158
Child psychiatry 107–20
  changing role of 118–19
  epidemiology in 113
  pivotal concepts in 116–18
  research 118–20
  scientific approach 109
  scientific tradition in 108–9
  see also Mental disorder in children
Child-rearing methods 24
Childhood fears 24
Chlordiazepoxide 17
Chlorpromazine 10, 89, 97
Cholecystokinin 150
Cirrhosis of the liver 40–41
Civil court proceedings 154
Clinical techniques 69–84
Clorazepate 17
Cocaine 60
Community care 163–71
Community psychiatric service 57–58
Community treatment programme 168, 169
Compulsive behaviour 31

Index

Compulsive gamblers 31
Computerised axial tomography (CAT scan) 42, 82, 101, 149
Computerised EEG (CEEG) 101–2
Conditional reflexes 75
Congenital malformations 124
Consultant psychiatrist 8
Consultation 118
Conversion hysteria 15
Convulsions 45
Counselling 33, 45, 46
Cretinism 124–27, 133
Creuzfeldt-Jakob's disease 144, 145
Criminal behaviour 153, 156
Criminal court cases 154
Criminal law 155
Criminal Law Revision Committee 156
Criminal offenders 161
Criminal responsibility 154–6
Crisis intervention service 170
Cushing's disease 60

Dalmane 17
Day Hospital 7
Delinquent behaviour 158
Delusions 137
Dementia 8, 42, 137
  causation of 139
  clinical observations 138
  clinical presentation, course and outcome 138
  due to infective process 143–45
  due to strokes 139, 143
  rare form of 147–48
  scientific investigation of 148
  senile 138, 139, 140, 142, 150, 151
  threshold concept 139–42
  treatment today or tomorrow 145–47
Dementia praecox 85
Depression 29, 59–68, 77, 137
  and suicide 49–53, 56–57
  bipolar 61, 67
  causes of 59
  chemical factors in 62
  constitutional factors in 59
  endogenous 18, 49, 50, 59, 61–63
  general management of 57
  genetic factors in 61
  incidence of 2
  nature of 59
  neurotic 16, 62
  pathological 59
  primary 52, 53, 61
  reactive 59
  recurrent 56
  treatment of 56, 62–67
  unipolar 61
Depressive illness 10, 48, 49
Depressive spectrum disorders 61
Dermatitis 76
Developing countries 168
Diabetes 140
Diagnosis
  advances in 3–5
  quality of 4
  realiability of 3
  uniformity of 4
Diazepam 16, 17
Diminished responsibility notion 155
Disadvantaged families 114
Dopamine 98–100
Dopamine receptors 100
Down's syndrome 141

Drug abuse 80
Drug addiction 3, 161, 170
Drug revolution 6
Drug therapy 9–10, 16–19, 29, 32, 63–67, 80–81, 89, 90, 92, 94, 97–99, 137, 143
see also under specific drugs
Drug trials 10, 28, 66

EEG 73, 74, 76, 101, 159
Electroshock treatment (ECT) 6, 57, 60, 62–64, 80
Emotional disorders 137
Encephalitis 146
Encephalitis lethargica 104
Environmental factors. *See* Social environment
Enzyme deficiency 128, 130
Epilepsy 74–76, 128
  temporal lobe 72–76
Ethical Committees 10, 65
Euhypnos 17
Exhibitionism 160
Exposure treatments 22
Expressed Emotion (EE) 93–95

Fainting 15
Family burden ratings 166–68
Family therapy 118–19
Fears. *See* Anxiety
Fetal Alcohol Syndrome 42
Fetishism 74
Financial restrictions 132–33
Financial support 9
Flurazepam 17
Forensic psychiatry 153–62

General Health Questionnaire 5
General paralysis of the insane (GPI) 69–71
Genetic disorders 122
Genetic factors 15, 61, 103, 122
Geriatric patients 3, 7
Glucose tolerance 140
Grendon Underwood prison 156–57
Grieving 16
Group therapy 26, 29, 46
Growth-restricting factors 128
Growth spurt 128, 130
Guam island 147
Guam Parkinsonism dementia 148
Guam Syndrome 148

Halcion 17
Hallucinations 45, 77, 86, 137
Heart rate 15
Heminevrin 45
Hereditary conditions and factors 12, 15, 89, 122, 127, 147
Herpes simplex 146
Home Care patients 169
Homicide Act 1957 155
Homosexuality 160
Hormonal effects 60, 83
Hospital admission 7–8, 166–67
Hospital Care patients 169
Hospital Friends associations 169
Hostile behaviour 137
Huntington's Chorea 142
Hydrocephalus 124
Hypnotics 55
Hypotensive drugs 140
Hypothyroidism 126, 127, 133, 145

Imaginal desensitisation procedure 31
Imipramine 10, 63, 64
Incest 160
Indecent exposure 160
Industrial countries 169
Insomnia 17, 33, 49
Intellectual deterioration 100
Intelligence 135
Intelligence quotient (IQ) 121–22, 126, 129
Intelligence scales 121
Intelligence tests 82
International Classification of Diseases 4, 5
International Pilot Study of Schizophrenia (IPSS) 87, 88
Iodine deficiency 125
Iproniazid 10, 64

Korsakoff's Syndrome 42
Kuru 144, 145

Laboratory techniques 11, 69–84
Librium 17
Life events 90–92
Lithium clinics 56–57
Lithium treatment 6, 10, 66, 67
Liver cirrhosis 40–41
Lorazepam 17

McNaughton Rules 155
Malformations 124
Malnutrition 41
Management of the mentally ill 6–8
Manic-depressive disorder 6, 10, 48–49, 51, 52, 54, 61, 66
Marital problems 28–29, 40
Masturbation 108

Maternal deprivation 12
Medazepam 17
Melancholics 6, 10
Memory impairment 143
Mental disorder
  causes of 78–81
  in children 107–20
    classification of 110–12
    diagnosis 111
    environmental component 119
    incidence of 108
    prevention of 108, 119–20
    public education 119–20
    research role 108
    treatment assessment 108
  see also Child psychiatry
  in old age. *See* Old age
  in prisoners 156–58
  see also Mental illness
Mental handicap 121–34
  causation of 122–23
  environmental factors 122–23
  genetic factors 122
  in children 3
  investigation of 121
  prevention of 124, 133
  research implications 131–32
Mental Health Act (1959) 7
Mental Health Foundation 166, 170
Mental hospitals 6
Mental illness
  distribution in the community 5
  incidence of 1–3
  present situation in 2–3
  prognosis for 2, 12
  see also Mental disorder
Mental retardation 112

Mentally disordered
    offenders 156
Metabolic disorders 76–77, 123
Mianserin 18
MIND 170
Mogadon 17
Monoamine oxidase
    inhibitors (MAOIs) 18, 64
Murder cases 155, 159

Nardil 16
National Health Service 6, 27, 157, 158
National Schizophrenic
    Fellowship 170
Nerve cells 141, 142
Neurofibrillary tangles 140–41
Neuroleptic drugs 97–99
Neuroses 14, 33, 137
    causation of 15, 16
    drug treatment of 16–19
    origins and treatment of 14–25
    prevalence of 14–15
    research 24
Neurotic depression 16, 62
Neurotransmitters 11, 60, 64, 149
Newcastle Scale 62
Nicotinamide 77, 78
Nitrazepam 17
Nobrium 17
Non-accidental injury in
    children 114–16, 159
Noradrenaline 61
Norepinephrine 150
Normison 17
Norval 18

Obsessive-compulsive
    rituals 20–23

Occupational therapy 6–7
Offenders
    sexually deviant 160
    treatment of 156–58
Old age 135–52
    advances in treatment of 151
    bitterness of 136
    clinical observations 138
    future research
        perspectives 148–52
    incidence of mental
        disorder 136
    neurochemistry 149
    problems of 135
    treatable and chronic
        illnesses in 136–38
Operational definitions 5
Overactive child 107
Oxazepam 17

Paedophilia 160
Palpitations 15
Panic 24
Paper chromatography 78
Parasuicide 3
Parkinson's disease 98, 142
Pellagra 76
Penicillin 9, 72
Peptides 11
Personality 135
Personality disorder 29
Personality studies 160
Personality test 53
Phenelzine 16, 63
Phenothiazines 6, 80, 81
Phenylalanine 78, 128–31
Phenylketonuria 78, 124, 127–31, 133
Phobias 22–23
    response to 15
Phobic disorder 14
Phobic relatives 16
Physical handicap 135

Index

Physical health standard 1
Plaque formation 141, 148
Pregnancy
   and alcohol abuse 42–43
   environmental factors 124
   phenylketonurics 131
Pregnancy tests 124
Premature senility 139
Present State Examination
   (PSE) 5, 87, 88
Prison sentence 155
Probation Services 157
Psychiatric disorder
   definition 112
   in children 112
      prevalence of 112–14
Psychiatric Hospital 166
Psychiatric illness 32
Psychiatric patients 7
Psychiatric services 32
Psychoanalysis 27, 30
Psychopathic personality
   157, 160
Psychosis, incidence of 12
Psychotherapy
   human component 27
   in general practice 32
   negative effects 29–30
   professional component
      27
   research 26–34
   structural characteristics
      of 26
Psychotic patients 6
Psychotropic drugs 33

Radio-immuno-assay 83
Reduced legal responsibility
   concept 154
Relaxation 23
   instruction in 33
Research advances 8–13
   see also under specific
      conditions

Research workers 9
Reserpine 64
'Revolving door' process 8
Role performance 167
Royal College of
      Psychiatrists 109, 170
Rubella embryopathy 122

Samaritans 56, 170
Schizophrenia 74, 85–106
   brain degeneration in
      100–3
   brain structural changes
      100–2
   causation of 12, 80, 91,
      103–6
   drug treatment 92, 94, 97
   emotional interaction in
      92–95
   first rank symptoms 86
   genetic factors 103
   incidence of 2, 5, 105
   inheritance of 89
   life events in 90–92
   nature of 85–87, 94
   neurochemistry of 99–100
   neuropathological
      changes 105
   neurotransmission
      disturbance 99–103
   pathology of 102
   present position in 86
   psychological changes 105
   psychological symptoms
      86
   research 105
   social influences 87–92, 95
   symptoms of 101
   syndromes in 102–3
   treatment of 10, 80, 97–99
   type I syndrome 103
   type II syndrome 103
   use of term 88
   viral aetiology 104

Schizophrenia Association 170
Scopolamine 143
Scrapie 145
Self-help 21, 22
Senescence 136
Serenid 17
Severe mental illness 155
Severe subnormality 155
Sexual behaviour 108
Sexual difficulties 21, 28
Sexual disorders 15
Sexual performance 14
Sexual violence 160
Sexually deviant offenders 160
Shoplifters 161
Side-effects 98
Sleeping tablets 16–18
Social environment 1, 12, 15, 39, 53–54, 87–92, 95, 119, 122–24
Social isolation 16
Social services 1
Sodium content 59
Sodium transport 60
Somatostatin 150
Soneryl 17
Special Hospital 155, 158
Special Hospital Research Unit 158
Standard lists and descriptions 4
Standard mortality ratio 41
Stanford-Binet scale 121
Storage diseases 124
Stress effects 14, 22, 92, 94–95, 107
Strokes 139, 140, 143
Suicide 48–58
  and alcohol 49, 55
  and depression 49–53, 56–57
  clinical postmortem 48–49
  incidence of 3, 56
  predisposing factors 48, 53–54
  resident psychiatric patients 57
  socio-cultural environment 53–54
Suicide attempts 51–54, 167
Suicide prevention 54–58
Suicide research 48
Suicide risk 53–57, 62
Suicide threat 55
Supportive psychotherapy 22
Syphilis 71–72

Technological advances 81–83
Temazepam 17
Temporal lobe epilepsy 72–76, 80
  with fetishism 74
Tension 22
Thalidomide 124
Thyroid deficiency 126
Thyrotropin 126
Thyroxin 126, 127
Toxic-infective psychoses 10
Tranquillisers 16–18, 55
Transsexualism 160
Transvestism 160
Tranxene 17
Trauma 16
Treatment 6–8
  see also under specific conditions
Triazolam 17
Tricyclic antidepressant drugs 6, 10, 18, 64, 67
Tryptizol 16
Tryptophan 77
Tryptophan break-down product 60
Turning Point 170

Index

Twin studies 12, 103

Urine tests 77

Vagrants 161
Valium 16, 17, 45
Violent behaviour 158–61
Vitamin B$_2$ 77
Vitamin B$_{12}$ deficiency 146
Voluntary organisations 170

Von Economo's disease 104

Wasserman reaction 71–72
Wechsler scale 121
Wellcome Trust 170
Willpower, scientific
 approach to 21
Worry 14

X-chromosome 61
X-rays 81, 149